An Analysis of

John Lewis Gaddis's

We Now Know
Rethinking Cold War History

Scott Gilfillan
with
Jason Xidias

www.macat.com
info@macat.com

Cover illustration: Etienne Gilfillan

Cataloguing in Publication Data
A catalogue record for this book is available from the British Library.
Library of Congress Cataloguing-in-Publication Data is available upon request.

ISBN 978-1-912302-56-7 (hardback)
ISBN 978-1-912128-13-6 (paperback)
ISBN 978-1-912281-44-2 (e-book)

Notice
The information in this book is designed to orientate readers of the work under analysis,
to elucidate and contextualise its key ideas and themes, and to aid in the development
of critical thinking skills. It is not meant to be used, nor should it be used, as a
substitute for original thinking or in place of original writing or research. References and
notes are provided for informational purposes and their presence does not constitute
endorsement of the information or opinions therein. This book is presented solely for
educational purposes. It is sold on the understanding that the publisher is not engaged
to provide any scholarly advice. The publisher has made every effort to ensure that
this book is accurate and up-to-date, but makes no warranties or representations with
regard to the completeness or reliability of the information it contains. The information
and the opinions provided herein are not guaranteed or warranted to produce particular
results and may not be suitable for students of every ability. The publisher shall not be
liable for any loss, damage or disruption arising from any errors or omissions, or from
the use of this book, including, but not limited to, special, incidental, consequential or
other damages caused, or alleged to have been caused, directly or indirectly, by the
information contained within.

CONTENTS

THE MACAT LIBRARY

The Macat Library is a series of unique academic explorations of seminal works in the humanities and social sciences – books and papers that have had a significant and widely recognised impact on their disciplines. It has been created to serve as much more than just a summary of what lies between the covers of a great book. It illuminates and explores the influences on, ideas of, and impact of that book. Our goal is to offer a learning resource that encourages critical thinking and fosters a better, deeper understanding of important ideas.

Each publication is divided into three Sections: Influences, Ideas, and Impact. Each Section has four Modules. These explore every important facet of the work, and the responses to it.

This Section-Module structure makes a Macat Library book easy to use, but it has another important feature. Because each Macat book is written to the same format, it is possible (and encouraged!) to cross-reference multiple Macat books along the same lines of inquiry or research. This allows the reader to open up interesting interdisciplinary pathways.

To further aid your reading, lists of glossary terms and people mentioned are included at the end of this book (these are indicated by an asterisk [*] throughout) – as well as a list of works cited.

Macat has worked with the University of Cambridge to identify the elements of critical thinking and understand the ways in which six different skills combine to enable effective thinking.
Three allow us to fully understand a problem; three more give us the tools to solve it. Together, these six skills make up the **PACIER** model of critical thinking. They are:

ANALYSIS – understanding how an argument is built
EVALUATION – exploring the strengths and weaknesses of an argument
INTERPRETATION – understanding issues of meaning

CREATIVE THINKING – coming up with new ideas and fresh connections
PROBLEM-SOLVING – producing strong solutions
REASONING – creating strong arguments

To find out more, visit **WWW.MACAT.COM.**

CRITICAL THINKING AND *WE NOW KNOW*

Primary critical thinking skill: EVALUATION
Secondary critical thinking skill: INTERPRETATION

John Lewis Gaddis had written four previous books on the Cold War by the time he published *We Now Know* – so the main thrust of his new work was not so much to present new arguments as to re-examine old ones in the light of new evidence that began emerging from behind the Iron Curtain after 1990. In this respect, *We Now Know* can be seen as an important exercise in evaluation; Gaddis not only undertook to reassess his own positions – arguing that this was the only intellectually honest course open to him in such changing circumstances – but also took the opportunity to address criticisms of his early works, not least by post-revisionist historians.

The straightforwardness and flexibility that Gaddis exhibited in consequence enhanced his book's authority. He also deployed interpretative skills to help him revise his methodology and reinterpret key historical arguments, integrating new, comparative histories of the Cold War era into his broader argument.

ABOUT THE AUTHOR OF THE ORIGINAL WORK

Born in the US state of Texas in 1941, **John Lewis Gaddis** is a prolific author, a respected academic, and a renowned Cold War expert. He has held professorships at the prestigious universities of Oxford, Yale, and Princeton, and won the 2012 Pulitzer Prize for his biography of American historian and diplomat George Kennan. He is currently Robert A. Lovett Professor of Military and Naval History at Yale University, and has been awarded the National Humanities Medal for deepening America's understanding of the humanities.

ABOUT THE AUTHORS OF THE ANALYSIS

Scott Gilfillan is a doctoral candidate in international history at the London School of Economics

Dr Jason Xidias holds a PhD in European Politics from King's College London, where he completed a comparative dissertation on immigration and citizenship in Britain and France. He was also a Visiting Fellow in European Politics at the University of California, Berkeley. Currently, he is Lecturer in Political Science at New York University.

ABOUT MACAT

GREAT WORKS FOR CRITICAL THINKING

Macat is focused on making the ideas of the world's great thinkers accessible and comprehensible to everybody, everywhere, in ways that promote the development of enhanced critical thinking skills.

It works with leading academics from the world's top universities to produce new analyses that focus on the ideas and the impact of the most influential works ever written across a wide variety of academic disciplines. Each of the works that sit at the heart of its growing library is an enduring example of great thinking. But by setting them in context – and looking at the influences that shaped their authors, as well as the responses they provoked – Macat encourages readers to look at these classics and game-changers with fresh eyes. Readers learn to think, engage and challenge their ideas, rather than simply accepting them.

'Macat offers an amazing first-of-its-kind tool for interdisciplinary learning and research. Its focus on works that transformed their disciplines and its rigorous approach, drawing on the world's leading experts and educational institutions, opens up a world-class education to anyone.'

Andreas Schleicher
Director for Education and Skills, Organisation for Economic Co-operation and Development

'Macat is taking on some of the major challenges in university education ... They have drawn together a strong team of active academics who are producing teaching materials that are novel in the breadth of their approach.'

Prof Lord Broers,
former Vice-Chancellor of the University of Cambridge

'The Macat vision is exceptionally exciting. It focuses upon new modes of learning which analyse and explain seminal texts which have profoundly influenced world thinking and so social and economic development. It promotes the kind of critical thinking which is essential for any society and economy. This is the learning of the future.'

Rt Hon Charles Clarke, former UK Secretary of State for Education

'The Macat analyses provide immediate access to the critical conversation surrounding the books that have shaped their respective discipline, which will make them an invaluable resource to all of those, students and teachers, working in the field.'

Professor William Tronzo, University of California at San Diego

WAYS IN TO THE TEXT

KEY POINTS

- John Lewis Gaddis is one of the most important historians on the subject of the Cold War*—a period of tension between the Soviet Union* and the United States, and countries aligned with each, in the years 1947 to 1991.

- *We Now Know: Rethinking Cold War History*, published in 1997, discusses the causes of the Cold War, its structure, how it developed, and its place in international history.

- Gaddis's main argument is that both the United States and the Soviet Union became empires* after 1945; the difference between them was that the United States ruled other nations by consent while the Soviet Union ruled by coercion. He accuses the Soviet leader Joseph Stalin* of making the Cold War drag on.

Who Is John Lewis Gaddis?

John Lewis Gaddis, the author of *We Now Know* (1997), is one of the most important experts on the subject of the Cold War. He was born in the city of Cotulla, Texas in 1941, and received a PhD from the University of Texas at Austin in 1968. After earning his doctorate, he taught at Indiana University Southeast before working at Ohio University from 1969 to 1997. He then moved on to Yale University, where he became Robert A. Lovett Professor of Military and Naval History, a position he still holds today. Gaddis has also held visiting professorships at the Naval War College, Oxford University, and Princeton University.

Gaddis's books include *The United States and the Origins of the Cold War, 1941–1947* (1972), *Strategies of Containment: A Critical Appraisal of Postwar American National Security* (1982), *The Long Peace: Inquiries into the History of the Cold War* (1987), and *The Cold War* (2005). He also wrote the official biography of the American historian and diplomat George Kennan,* for which he won the Pulitzer Prize for Biography and the American History Book Prize in 2012.

Gaddis explains in the book's preface that *We Now Know* came from a series of eight lectures he gave at Oxford University in 1992 while spending a year there as a visiting professor. For Gaddis, it was a fascinating time to be involved in Cold War research, as the period had only just come to an end: "This was the first full year of what everyone agreed was the post-Cold War era," he said, "and, as a consequence, my first opportunity to lecture on the Cold War from beginning to end."[1]

What Does *We Now Know* Say?

John Lewis Gaddis's *We Now Know* looks at our historical understanding of the Cold War from a new, international perspective. The main goal of the text is to show readers that new documentary evidence from the former Soviet Union, Eastern Europe, and China has changed the historiography* of the Cold War—that is, the way histories of the Cold War have been written.

Gaddis argues that these new documents have to be taken into account if you want to explain the Cold War as international history. He calls this "new Cold War history."[2] This new historiographical approach, he says, means we can now answer questions such as: Who started the Cold War? Why did it escalate? Why did it last so long? And why did it end?

The main ideas in *We Now Know* spring from the opportunity created by the appearance of the new source material. Gaddis argues in the text that such new documentary evidence obliged historians to revisit many of the traditional arguments about the Cold War and to compare materials from everywhere to get a new, international, view of the period's history.

Gaddis's new way of looking at the Cold War all leads to the book's last chapter, "The New Cold War History: First Impressions," which sums up the text's key ideas. In eight short hypotheses about "what we now know," representing a significant departure from his previous understanding of Cold War history, Gaddis condenses all the points on specific Cold War events that he covers in the previous nine chapters.

During the 1970s and 1980s, Gaddis had become a well-known member of the post-revisionist* school of Cold War history. Post-revisionist historians wanted to go beyond the usual arguments about the origins of the Cold War towards interpretations that stressed the importance of geopolitics*—that is, politics influenced by geographical factors, such as where things are, what resources they have, the balances of power between nations, and so on. Gaddis had argued that the balance of power between the US and the Soviet Union as well as the focus on grand strategy*—that is, the strategic use of all the financial, diplomatic and cultural means open to a nation in pursuit of some aim—were both essential elements in US-Soviet policymaking and were responsible for making the Cold War last as long as it did.

What Gaddis discovered when researching *We Now Know* forced him to rethink previous ideas. "The diversification of power did more to shape the course of the Cold War than did the balancing of power,"[3] he argues in the book's concluding chapter—by which he means that the Americans had built a democratic empire superior to the autocratic (that is, dictatorial and repressive) Soviet empire. He also concludes "that as long as Joseph Stalin was running the Soviet Union, a cold war was unavoidable."[4]

According to the Norwegian Cold War historian Odd Arne Westad, these ideas were "a return to some of the concerns—but not always the conclusions—of Cold War orthodoxy."[5] Gaddis did not expect his new theories, which contradicted his previous thought, to stay true forever, and he predicted that future histories would probably go on to challenge his "new Cold War history" as more evidence became available.

Why Does *We Now Know* Matter?

We Now Know argues that the new documentary evidence that had come from the former Soviet Union and its allies since the end of the Cold War changed how the conflict should be understood historically. The title of the book is important, as the main aim of *We Now Know* was to explain what "we"—that is, Gaddis and his readers—"now know" about the Cold War. The title was an invitation to readers to join Gaddis on a journey through the new history of the Cold War. The author's interpretation of the new documents and evidence would make it clear what he believed people now knew about the Cold War (as opposed what people thought they knew before this evidence was available), why it started, how it escalated and why it went on for so long.

When *We Now Know* was published, it was an exciting time for Cold War research. The consensus view was that the collapse of the Soviet Union meant an end to the Cold War, allowing the first histories of the entire period of conflict to be written. And, given the slew of new documents from the former Soviet Union and its allies in Eastern Europe and China, researchers had the opportunity to write histories from a fully international perspective. This, of course, had a significant effect on both Gaddis's decision to write *We Now Know* and on the conclusions that he came to—as he admits in the book's preface, acknowledging the debt he owed to the work of other historians in the course of researching and writing his study.

We Now Know is a landmark work on the struggle for political and ideological supremacy between the United States and the Soviet Union during the second half of the twentieth century. Looking at the conflict from its early beginnings through to the Cuban Missile Crisis* of October 1962 (the closest the Cold War came to a "hot" war fought with nuclear weapons), its use of newly available documents from both Western and communist nations and its novel interpretation of events establish it as a key work of so-called "new Cold War history."

NOTES

1   John Lewis Gaddis, *What We Now Know: Rethinking Cold War History* (Oxford: Clarendon Press, 1997), preface, vii.

2   Gaddis, *We Now Know*, preface, viii.

3   Gaddis, *We Now Know*, 283.

4   Gaddis, *We Now Know*, 284–5, 292.

5   Odd Arne Westad, "Bibliographical Essay: The Cold War and the International History of the Twentieth Century," in *The Cambridge History of the Cold War, Volume 1: Origins*, eds. Melvyn P. Leffler and Odd Arne Westad (Cambridge: Cambridge University Press, 2010), 509.

SECTION 1
INFLUENCES

MODULE 1
THE AUTHOR AND THE HISTORICAL CONTEXT

KEY POINTS

- *We Now Know* provided a fresh historical interpretation of the period of tension between the United States and its allies and the Soviet Union and its allies known as the Cold War.*
- The main focus of John Lewis Gaddis's lifelong research has been the Cold War. He is considered one of the leading experts on the subject.
- Gaddis wrote the book in the mid-1990s, a period when the world was adjusting to a new system of international relations ushered in by the end of the Cold War and when common understandings of historical event were being challenged.

Why Read This Text?

John Lewis Gaddis's *We Now Know,* published in 1997, is essential reading for anyone interested in the Cold War as well as international history more broadly. Gaddis wrote it after the collapse of Soviet communism*—a social and economic ideology originally founded on concepts such as the common ownership of industry and the abolition of class—and set out to provide a historical explanation for that collapse.

In the text, the author brings together newly–available primary and secondary sources to present a detailed assessment and fresh understanding of the conflict between America and the Soviet Union. ("Primary sources" are usually original documents or testimony;

> ❝ By 'now,' I seek to situate this book at a particular point in time, not to claim timelessness for it. This is what I think we know now but did not know, or at least did not know as clearly, while the Cold War was going on. ❞
>
> John Lewis Gaddis, *We Now Know: Rethinking Cold War History*

"secondary sources" include commentary and analysis.) Gaddis does this through an examination of the Cuban Missile Crisis* of 1962, a short period of grave diplomatic tension that almost led to a nuclear war. His focus, in other words, is on the first third of the Cold War.

Gaddis sees the outbreak of the Cold War as a result of the power vacuum that World War II created in Europe with all the former major powers effectively neutralized. And he blames the fact that it went on so long mainly on Stalinism*—the aggressive political doctrine of the Soviet leader Joseph Stalin who, Gaddis claims, craved conflict and looked for it wherever he could.

Gaddis pinpoints the start of the Cold War as 1947, the moment when it became obvious to the American government that the Soviets were unwilling to cooperate in a multilateral global order—that is, an agreed-on international system—that the US wanted to lead.

As far as the Cuban Missile Crisis was concerned, Gaddis argues in *We Now Know* that Soviet leader Nikita Khrushchev* looked to safeguard communist Cuba, headed by the revolutionary leader Fidel Castro,* by putting nuclear missiles there. He also argues that the conflict would have escalated had not the US president John F. Kennedy* sought compromise and peace. He goes on to suggest that the reason it did not end much earlier, bearing in mind how the Soviet Union declined economically, was that both countries had nuclear weapons. He also says that the arms race created a balance of power in international politics that may have prevented a third World War.

Gaddis's detailed presentation in *We Now Know* created what he calls "a new Cold War history": a novel approach to the historical period that offered new insights and laid the foundation for further study and debate on the subject.

Author's Life

John Lewis Gaddis was born in the town of Cotulla, Texas in 1941 and began his academic career at the University of Texas at Austin. After finishing his doctorate there under the supervision of Robert Divine,* a scholar of diplomatic history and the US presidency, Gaddis briefly worked as a researcher and teacher at Indiana University Southeast before moving on to the University of Ohio, where he stayed until 1997—the year he published *We Now Know*. Today, he is Robert A. Lovett Professor of Military and Naval History at Yale University and is widely regarded as one of the leading historians of the Cold War.

Gaddis has also held visiting professorships at the Naval War College, Oxford University, Princeton University, and the University of Helsinki. During his academic career, he has received several important accolades, including the Pulitzer Prize and the National Humanities Medal.

We Now Know came from eight lectures that Gaddis gave as a visiting professor at Oxford University in 1992. Drawing on documents fresh from the archives, he came up with a new way of looking at the causes of the Cold War, as well as its structure, development, and place in international history. The text is thought of as one of the seminal works on the subject.

Author's Background

Gaddis initially set out only to rewrite his lecture notes, putting them in the perspective of international history rather than simply the history of United States diplomacy. But as new documents from the former Soviet Union, the People's Republic of China, and Eastern

Europe became available, he decided that the time was right to write "a comprehensive history of the Cold War that would incorporate as much of this new material as possible while relating it to what we already knew."[1]

Due to the sheer volume of documents relating to the early years of the Cold War, Gaddis decided to focus on the first third of that conflict—which is why he organized *We Now Know* into a series of overlapping but connected histories extending through the Cuban Missile Crisis. He wrote the book in the mid-1990s, when the world was adjusting to a post–Cold-War system of international relations. At that time, people began contesting many concepts that had been previously accepted about Cold War history, such as the idea that the Soviet Union was responsible for the conflict as a result of its attempt to spread communism through Eastern Europe.

Influenced by new histories of the Cold War, Gaddis decided to write a book that would bring the latest historical research together into a single volume. The result was *We Now Know*, a groundbreaking work that pioneered the approach of "new Cold War" history. The book is still relevant to students of the Cold War today.

NOTES

1   John Lewis Gaddis, *What We Now Know: Rethinking Cold War History* (Oxford: Clarendon Press, 1997), preface, vii.

ACADEMIC CONTEXT

KEY POINTS

- In *We Now Know*, John Lewis Gaddis used new primary sources and put them together with existing literature to provide a fresh interpretation of Cold War* history.

- Gaddis focused on the first third of the Cold War. This approach differed from other historians who either assessed the Cold War as one important part of a larger history or focused on one Cold War event, such as the Cuban Missile Crisis* of 1962.

- Although the author worked in a similar way to the Cold War historian Louis Halle,* who had published an important work of Cold War history in 1967, Gaddis had two important advantages over Halle: he knew the outcome of the conflict, and he had access to new sources of information from the Soviet Union, China, and Eastern Europe.

The Work in its Context

John Gaddis Lewis was one of several historians who were aiming to provide a new international history of the Cold War. In the book's preface, he acknowledges the debt of gratitude that he owes to the many young scholars writing the so-called "new Cold War history"— to which *We Now Know* was to make a vital contribution. Gaddis's approach was novel, however, in that his ambition was to write a full history of the first third of the Cold War and not just the story of one event within it, such as the Cuban Missile Crisis.

At the time of the book's publication, people were very interested in making sense of the events of the Cold War and considering what its

> 66 The end of the Cold War brought a widely-acknowledged era to an end. New evidence has continued to be uncovered in the United States; but the opening of the Soviet archives especially has offered a trove of materials. This has given rise to a 'new Cold War history' as younger scholars have mined Soviet documents to write the studies produced by the Cold War International History Project. 99
>
> Howard H. Lentner,* "New Cold War History: A Review of *We Now Know: Rethinking Cold War History*"

end meant for the future of international politics. "New Cold War history" was uncharted territory. To find answers to the field's pressing questions, Gaddis turned to fresh sources from the archives of the Soviet Union, China, and Eastern Europe. He questioned everything that anyone had previously written on the subject, including his own scholarly contributions. After writing *We Now Know*, he came to see international history in a very different way—as did those who read it.

Overview of the Field

When the Cold War came to an end, many historians wanted to make use of new material that was coming to light. The immediate post-Cold War period was an exciting time for these scholars. Some, such as the British historian Eric Hobsbawm,* chose to write about how ideas and ideologies progressed throughout the whole twentieth century, while others chose to think of the Cold War as a conflict that began in 1917 with the Russian Revolution,* rather than after World War II in 1947.

Although the Cold War's end and the availability of a great quantity of documents prompted a surge in historical writing and study, Gaddis successfully incorporated much of this newly available material and analysis into his book in a readable and coherent fashion. In its preface, Gaddis acknowledges the rapid change that was taking place in the discipline and admits it was highly likely that many of the book's conclusions would be questioned as more documents came to light. He takes pains to stress that the "now" in the title was only supposed "to situate the book at a particular point in time, not to claim timelessness for it."[1]

While some of Gaddis's ideas have come under critical scrutiny since the book's publication, the text remains one of the most important works on Cold War history.

Academic Influences

In the preface to *We Now Know*, Gaddis explains that he set out to follow the example of Louis Halle's classic book *The Cold War As History* (1967).[2] According to that work, the confrontation between the United States and the Soviet Union should be viewed: "as a phenomenon not without precedent in the long history of international conflict; as a phenomenon that, experience has taught us, has its own dynamics; as a phenomenon that, typically, goes through a certain cycle with a beginning, a middle, and an end."[3]

Gaddis then explains that he had two advantages over Halle. First, as the Cold War had just ended, Gaddis knew the outcome; and second, he had access to new documents from the Soviet Union, China, and Eastern Europe. With this, he hoped to come up with a new understanding of Cold War history based on connected and overlapping histories of the conflict.

The author's experience at Oxford University also helped shape the book. It grew out a series of lectures that he delivered there as a visiting scholar. Gaddis credits Tim Barton of Oxford University Press, who he came into contact with during his stay, as the first person to suggest that he should turn those lectures into a book.[4] He completed parts of his research and writing at the National Security Archive and the Woodrow Wilson Center* in the United States (an American institution dedicated to research and communication in the field of US world affairs) and the Norwegian Nobel Institute. He then presented his chapters and received valuable feedback on them at the Council on Foreign Relations, a non-governmental research and advocacy organization concerned with US foreign policy that is based in New York.

NOTES

1 John Lewis Gaddis, *What We Now Know: Rethinking Cold War History* (Oxford, Clarendon Press, 1997), preface, viii.

2 Louis Halle, *The Cold War As History* (New York: Harper and Row, 1967).

3 Cited in Gaddis, preface, vii.

4 Gaddis, ix.

THE PROBLEM

KEY POINTS

- John Lewis Gaddis wanted to find out whether comparing new archives from the Soviet Union, Eastern Europe, and China with those available in the United States and its allied countries would result in a new interpretation of Cold War* history.

- This methodological approach was novel because no one had compared this archival material until then.

- In *We Now Know*, Gaddis drew from resources fresh from the archives and recent secondary literature—that is, analysis written by other historians—to provide a full comparative account of the first third of the Cold War.

Core Question

Writing *We Now Know*, Gaddis wanted to find out whether comparing new documentary source material from the archives of the former Soviet Union, the People's Republic of China, and other countries in Eastern Europe with sources from the United States and its allies would change the historical understanding of the Cold War. That was a fundamentally important question at the time because, before the publication of *We Now Know*, there had not been a comprehensive, comparative history of the conflict that took into account the points of view of all of the principal players of the Cold War—or at least as many as possible.

In *We Now Know*, Gaddis tackles this challenge by approaching the subject matter in a highly detailed and methodical fashion. He focuses on the first third of the Cold War for two reasons: 1) he had more

> ❝ What is so distinctive about Gaddis's new book is the extent to which he abandons post-revisionism* and returns to a more traditional interpretation of the Cold War. In unequivocal terms, he blames the Cold War on Stalin's personality, on authoritarian government, and on Communist ideology. ❞
>
> Melvyn Leffler,* "Review Essay: The Cold War: What do 'We Now Know'?"

source material relating to that period, and 2) he was able to make use of many new English language works devoted to that part of the Cold War. Gaddis's chapter-by-chapter breakdown of the major developments of the early Cold War in *We Now Know* leads to a concluding chapter that condenses his analysis into eight short ideas that, he argues, form the tenets of "new Cold War history"—an influential new way of interpreting the events of the Cold War.

The Participants

At the time of publication, many other scholars were also attempting to come to terms with the history of the Cold War and what its end meant for the world. The historians Vladislav Zubok* and Constantine Pleshakov,* for example, focused on the intricacies of Russian decision-making. Others concentrated on subjects like China's role in the Korean War,* a conflict fought by North and South Korea between 1950 and 1953 with significant interventions from the United States and communist China.[1] But *We Now Know* stood out among the glut of new histories that appeared around the same time because, instead of examining one particular element, it set out to adopt a comprehensive international approach to the whole first third of the Cold War. For that reason, it appealed to a much broader audience.

The book was a natural progression from the earlier academic work that Gaddis had done in the field of Cold War history. As one of the pioneers of post-revisionist* Cold War history, an approach that questioned the recent orthodoxy of the United State's role in provoking and continuing the conflict, Gaddis had already started to work in a way that compared histories in various countries in his study of the Cold War.[2] The definitive end of the Cold War in 1991 allowed him to apply this way of working to the flood of new documents that had begun to emerge from the East.

Thus, he became the first Cold War historian to put together how the struggle unfolded from both sides of the ideological divide, the West (the United States and its allies), on one hand, and the East (the Soviet Union and its allies), on the other.

The Contemporary Debate

The text is quite closely related to other works on the period published in the late 1990s, in that it aimed to look anew at the history of the Cold War. Gaddis was clear about the fact that the work owed a great deal to new source material and newly published research. He was especially open about his use of the *Bulletins* and working papers of the Cold War International History Project at the Woodrow Wilson Center* in Washington. Indeed, each chapter of the book refers to well-known work of other scholars to tell its story.

In chapter three, "Cold War Empires: Asia," for example, Gaddis makes frequent use of studies by, among many others, the Norwegian historian Odd Arne Westad* on the Chinese Civil War,* the historians Jian Chen* and William Stueck* on the Korean War,* and Shu Guang Zhang on Sino-American relations[3] and the communist ideology of the Chinese revolutionary leader Mao Zedong.*[4]

If *We Now Know* considered the ideas and analyses of many other writers, it did not necessarily go along with their conclusions, however. In fact, the reason why *We Now Know* became a key example of the "new Cold War history" was that it drew the contributions of many other historians together into a coherent whole that became the first comprehensive comparative account of the first third of the Cold War. Gaddis used secondary texts—that is, analysis and commentary—to construct the story he was telling and to provide insightful source material. But the conclusions he drew were entirely his own.

NOTES

1   See in particular: Vladislav Zubok and Constantine Pleshakov, *Inside the Kremlin's Cold War: From Stalin to Khrushchev* (Cambridge, MA: Harvard University Press, 1996); and Shu Guang Zhang, *Mao's Military Romanticism: China and the Korean War, 1950–1953* (Lawrence: University Press of Kansas, 1995).

2   John Lewis Gaddis, *The United States and the Origins of the Cold War, 1941–1947* (New York: Colombia University Press, 1972); and John Lewis Gaddis, "The Emerging Post-Revisionist Synthesis on the Origins of the Cold War," *Diplomatic History 7*, No. 3 (1983): 131–48.

3   Shu Guang Zhang, *Deterrence and Strategic Culture: Chinese-American Confrontations, 1949–1958* (Ithaca: Cornell University Press, 1992).

4   Shu Guang Zhang, *Mao's Military Romanticism: China and the Korean War, 1950–1953* (Lawrence: University Press of Kansas, 1995).

MODULE 4
THE AUTHOR'S CONTRIBUTION

KEY POINTS

- In *We Now Know: Rethinking Cold War History* John Lewis Gaddis sought to present a new interpretation of Cold War* history based on the bringing together of new archives and current analysis.

- The book is structured into individual units that deal with either a prominent event or a geopolitical situation during the Cold War.

- He produced what he called a "new Cold War history"—and what remains a very important reference point on the subject.

Author's Aims

John Lewis Gaddis's *We Now Know* was aimed at scholars and fellow historians of the Cold War who were finding that older books written in the midst of the conflict were no longer sufficient.

Gaddis had already written many well-known histories of the Cold War. To give his new work credibility he had to question the post-revisionist* arguments in his own works (that is, the recently superseded consensus regarding the United States' imperial ambitions).

Although it may have been difficult for Gaddis to have to argue against what he had previously said in the light of new research, the bravery and flexibility it took gave him the credibility he needed to reach a wider audience and heightened the book's authority. Gaddis accepted his changing views as part of the natural process of studying history. He criticized those historians who would not adapt to the post-Cold-War world and continued to argue cases that the new documentary evidence had roundly contradicted.

> 66 This brilliant study—Gaddis' fifth book on the
> Cold War—provides an exhaustive and ever-quizzical
> approach to the early years of the superpower conflict. 99
> David Hendrickson,* "Review: *We Now Know: Rethinking Cold War History*"

As we have seen, Gaddis's main aim in writing *We Now Know* was to come up with the first "new Cold War history"—the term he used to describe the new, international, approach that compared documents from different sources to study the early period of the Cold War. In bringing together the historical theories about such an important and long-lasting event, Gaddis clearly hoped that *We Now Know* would become the definitive Cold War text for historians in a post-Cold War world. Every chapter of the book contains this underlying message; in each one, he uses his new methodology to revisit and reinterpret certain historical arguments. The aims of *We Now Know* demonstrate a coherent and clear plan with individual units based on a particular theme that deals with either a prominent event or a geopolitical situation during the Cold War. Gaddis offers a step-by-step analysis of the early conflict, with revised theories to explain his findings.

Approach

Gaddis wanted to rethink the way in which the Cold War was understood by comparing new documentary evidence coming from the former Soviet Union and its allies to the sources that already existed in the United States and Western Europe. This was partly an extension of the post-revisionist* methods that he had adopted earlier in his career.[1]

Post-revisionism,* also known as the "realist" approach, wanted to leave behind the revisionist* views of recent work in Cold War history, which focused on the ambitions of the United States to dominate global politics. It aimed to replace it with a comparative methodology—comparing material from different sources—that was less concerned with who should be blamed for the conflict.

Gaddis used documentary evidence from both sides to underline the importance of power balances in the international system and grand strategy* (roughly, the deliberate use of every diplomatic, financial, and cultural tool available to a nation that wants to pursue certain objectives in international affairs) in US–Soviet policymaking. According to Gaddis, these two things accounted for the length and stable character of the Cold War and helped to explain why the major players acted in the way that they did.[2]

That previous work put Gaddis in a good position to understand what the arrival of new documents from the Soviet Union Eastern Europe and China meant for Cold War history. For the first time, he was able to present a truly international account of what happened in the Cold War.

Contribution in Context

The main ideas that John Gaddis discusses in *We Now Know* go straight to the heart of the preoccupations of the historical period in which it was written.

At the time of its publication in 1997, a huge amount of new source material from the former countries of the Soviet Union and its allies had totally changed the debate about the Cold War in the United States and Western Europe. Historians were challenging historical interpretations that most people had previously agreed on. Instead of writing diplomatic accounts from the American or Western European point of view, as their predecessors had been forced to, the collapse of the Soviet Union meant that historians were able to write comparative international histories of a conflict that had finally ended.

Gaddis wanted to make the most of that opportunity. As he points out in the book, Cold War events largely defined the life of his generation and his research. He sets out to put all of this into practice by providing a fresh look at what the world had been living through.

Authors of related works have praised *We Now Know* for its breadth and ambition, even if they have not always agreed with its central arguments. For example, the historian Melvyn Leffler,* who had been a critic of Gaddis's earlier work, admitted that the book was "likely to set the parameters for a whole new generation of scholarship."[3]

NOTES

1   Gaddis published two seminal post-revisionist studies: John Lewis Gaddis, *Strategies of Containment: A Critical Appraisal of Postwar American National Security Policy* (New York: Oxford University Press, 1982); and John Lewis Gaddis, "The Emerging Post-Revisionist Synthesis on the Origins of the Cold War," *Diplomatic History 7*, No. 3 (1983): 131–148.

2   Odd Arne Westad, "The Cold War and the International History of the Twentieth Century," in *The Cambridge History of the Cold War*, Vol. 1, eds. Melvyn P. Leffler and Odd Arne Westad, eds. (Cambridge: Cambridge University Press, 2010), 5.

3   Melvyn P. Leffler, "The Cold War: What Do 'We Now Know'?" *The American Historical Review* 104, No. 2 (1999): 502.

SECTION 2
IDEAS

MAIN IDEAS

KEY POINTS

- The core proposal in *We Now Know: Rethinking Cold War History*, by John Lewis Gaddis, is that the Cold War* should be understood very differently than had previously been thought.

- Gaddis suggests throughout the text that his analysis will be subject to critiques and enhanced interpretations as new sources of information become available.

- In the book, he presents the reasons why the Cold War started, escalated, endured, and ended in 10 distinct, coherent chapters; in doing so, he establishes a novel framework for interpreting international history.

Key Themes

To John Lewis Gaddis, the end of the Cold War meant that historians had a duty "to account for the rise, flourishing, and decline of the Russian–American global hegemony."[1] (In the field of international relations, "hegemony" refers to dominance.) With *We Now Know*, he aimed to meet this obligation, asking whether the conflict had to happen in the first place and setting out a clear definition for a "new Cold War history" that future scholars could explore and debate.

But *We Now Know* was not just an examination of these general themes. Gaddis weaved his principal goal of presenting his new history into a much more detailed account of some of the most significant and controversial events of the early Cold War.

The book starts with the "vacuum of legitimacy"[2] in the system of international relations after World War I* that produced the 1917

❝ The Cold War in Gaddis's account was both inevitable and necessary. The Soviet empire and its allies could not be rolled back but they had to be contained. The resulting standoff lasted forty years. A lot of time and money was spent on nuclear weapons and the cautious new strategic thinking to which they gave rise. Partly for this reason there were no major wars. In the end—thanks to greater resources, a vastly more attractive political and economic model, and the initiative of a few good men (and one good woman)—the right side won. ❞

Tony Judt,* "A Story Still To Be Told"

Russian Revolution*—a revolution fought to replace the existing social and economic system in Russia with communism.* Gaddis argues that the two World Wars broke up the German, Austro-Hungarian, and Ottoman (or "Turkish") empires. Those wars also discredited old forms of diplomacy that were obviously unable to prevent large-scale conflict between nations. American and Russian ideologies and military power filled this void.

The book ends with the Cuban Missile Crisis in 1962,* a time when the United States and the Soviet Union seemed on the brink of nuclear war. The book covers a wide range of twentieth century history in its attempt to explain why the Cold War started, escalated, endured, and ended.

Gaddis explores different events and themes relating to the early Cold War in each chapter of *We Now Know*. Although he gives a separate historical account in each chapter, they all incorporate his general approach to his new Cold War history. The reader can understand Gaddis's central argument reading chapters individually or in sequence: that the new documentary evidence that has emerged since the end of the Cold War has raised serious questions about what had formerly been accepted as historical truths.[3]

Exploring the Ideas

Gaddis breaks the material down into subject areas, organizing content into 10 distinct chapters. The first nine chapters divide the Cold War into a series of geographical and conceptual themes, including imperialism* (the policy of empire building through military or cultural means), ideology, grand strategy,* the balance of power* (the stability brought about by an equal distribution of power in the international system), personalities, nuclear weaponry, alliances, and the Third World* (usually called "the developing world" today). Each chapter focuses on a different aspect of the Cold War in order to support Gaddis's central argument that some specific historical understanding needs to change.

The book starts with a look at the background of the great rivalry between the United States and the Soviet Union from the beginning of their existence. This led to the division of Europe into two Cold War empires, the borders of which soon spread to Asia. Gaddis argues that new evidence proved that the Soviet leader Joseph Stalin* played the main role in the beginning of the Cold War. He also says that once Stalin's ambitions in Europe had been thwarted, his romantic ideas about revolution turned to Korea, where they would eventually lead to war.

At this point, the development of nuclear weapons prolonged the Cold War, as the rivalry became narrowly based on military strength— hence, the Cuban missile crisis. Gaddis also covers other important regions, such as Germany and the developing nations of Asia, Africa, and Latin America, as well as the issue of what the new documents tell us about the ideology of the Cold War. In his opinion, these documents show that societies built on the principles of liberal democracy* and capitalism* (the dominant model of government, economy, and society in the West) were stronger and longer-lasting than those of Marxism-Leninism* (the political ideology on which the Soviet Union was founded).

The final chapter of *We Now Know* boils down what Gaddis means by the "new Cold War history." In it, Gaddis condenses the previous nine chapters into a series of short hypotheses, or theories, that "represent what I think we know *now* but did not know, at least not as clearly, while the Cold War was going on."[4] A series of bold statements follow about how the Cold War should be historically understood from here on out. The "new Cold War history" proves that the Cold War was basically a struggle between two imperialist superpowers—a contest between good and evil, and inevitable as long as Stalin controlled the Soviet Union. By stitching together the different themes of earlier chapters in such a powerful way, Gaddis makes it clear that when we look at the Cold War as international history, we should understand it in a completely different way than we had previously.

Language and Expression

As we have seen, Gaddis's arguments are neatly arranged into eight to-the-point hypotheses, or theories, each of which relates to conclusions made at the end of every chapter. This means that readers can get an idea of his position without having to read the entire book. Looking at *We Now Know* as a whole, we can see that it is not just a history of separate events, but also a fresh interpretation of the entire period.

To fully understand the arguments Gaddis makes on Cold War topics, such as the division of Europe or the Korean War,* however, the reader needs a firm grounding in revisionist* Cold War historiography*—that is, the written history that had come before, with its assumptions about the United States' role in perpetuating and provoking the conflict. To help students develop their own understanding of Cold War events, other sources are available on the website of the "Cold War International Project" at the Woodrow Wilson International Center for Scholars.*[5] These supplementary materials help us come to our own conclusions on some of the arguments that Gaddis presents on specific Cold War themes such as ideology, the balance of power, nuclear weapons and the developing world. They provide context on the general debates that we need to consider when studying history, such as the importance of circumstance or of the individual people who were involved in events.

NOTES

1   John Lewis Gaddis, *We Now Know: Rethinking Cold War History* (Oxford: Clarendon Press, 1997), 2.

2   Gaddis, *We Now Know*, 4.

3   In Cold War history, orthodox interpretations place responsibility for the Cold War on the Soviet Union because of its "Sovietization" of Eastern Europe and ambitions to spread Communism around the world.

4   Gaddis, *We Now Know*, 283.

5   The Cold War International History Project website can be found at: http://www.wilsoncenter.org/program/cold-war-international-history-project.

SECONDARY IDEAS

KEY POINTS

- The United States and Soviet Union had different imperialistic* traits. That is, each country used different strategies to build informal empires in Europe and Asia.

- The United States defended a doctrine of collective security, or an arrangement in which a group of nations promoted peace, The Russians sought to increase their security through territorial acquisitions.

- Critics argued that John Lewis Gaddis was too focused on showing that the American system, founded on liberal democracy* and a capitalist* economy, offered a social and economic model superior to that of Soviet communism.* They said that he paid too little attention to other actors who influenced the Cold War* apart from the United States and Soviet Union.

Other Ideas

Gaddis makes many important secondary arguments in *We Now Know*. From these arguments, developed in the first nine chapters, come the broader conclusions that he reaches in chapter 10.

To fully appreciate the overall thrust of his argument, then, readers should first try to understand the in-depth analysis in each chapter. They should look at all of these secondary ideas in the context of the new primary source documents from the archives of the former Soviet Union* and its allies—material that encouraged Gaddis to take an international approach to his analysis of the Cold War.

> ❝ That ideological euphoria ... diminished the caution that had shaped Stalin's previous behavior toward the United States. He thus allowed Kim Il-Sung to talk him into something he had earlier refused to do: authorizing an effort to reunify the Korean peninsula by military means. Mao, more skeptical, went along because of his own designs on Taiwan; but when the North Koreans began to lose, he too threw caution to the winds and confronted the Americans convinced that ideological zeal would ensure success. ❞
>
> John Lewis Gaddis, *We Now Know: Rethinking Cold War History*

The result is a way of looking at issues from both sides rather than just the American or Western European point of view.

The main secondary themes that Gaddis considers are the different types of alliances that the two superpowers formed. These were related to their opposing ideologies: in the West, society was founded on liberal democracy (a form of government in which leaders are regularly elected and individual liberty is secured) and capitalism (an economic model in which businesses and profits are in private hands); in the East, government was founded on Marxist-Leninism,* according to which individuals have little say in the nation's governance and the state owns and manages industry.

Gaddis further discusses in the text the important role that the Russian leader Joseph Stalin* played in prolonging the Cold War, the superpowers' different visions of European security, and how the threat of nuclear weapons helped create a balance of power* and stability in a state of international anarchy* (that is, the lack of any global government and authority).

Exploring the Ideas

Gaddis set out in *We Now Know* to show that when you compare the ideologically opposed alliances built by the United States and the Soviet Union, they both had similar, imperialistic* traits (that is, both adopted policies of empire building).

Even if they employed different methods, both the United States and the Soviet Union built informal empires in Europe and Asia, exerting their influence over huge populations outside their borders. Gaddis also describes how, after World War II,* the United States and the Soviet Union both wanted to ensure future peace in Europe—the difference was the *type* of peace each desired. The United States was in favor of collective security,* to be achieved by getting nations to join together, while the Soviet Union sought security through the acquisition of territory, bringing more countries under its influence. These arguments are not entirely original, but the way that Gaddis presents them, comparing American and Soviet sources, helps set *We Now Know* apart.

This is also true of what the book says about Asia. Gaddis contrasts Soviet policymaking—including how it was dependent on Stalin and his relationship with allies such as China's first communist leader Mao Zedong* and Kim Il-Sung,* his Korean equivalent—with the policymaking of the United States and its allies. Soviet blunders, he concludes, led to the escalation of the Cold War in Asia.

Gaddis also uses his comparative method to explore the struggle for control in the developing nations of Africa, Asia, and Latin America; the nuclear arms race; and the differing fortunes of each side's ideological alliance partners. This is a convincing approach, backed up by the extensive use of both primary and secondary source material. Each chapter strengthens the central arguments of the text, offers a stand-alone unit of research for the more focused scholar, and reinforces Gaddis's overall approach.

Overlooked

We Now Know is still a seminal text of Cold War history and has continued to attract attention from Cold War historians since its publication. For this reason, not much of the book has been overlooked in the writing of Cold War history. Gaddis covered some of the most important events of the Cold War in the text, looking in detail at important developments such as the division of Europe, the Korean War,* and the Cuban Missile Crisis.*

Since the book's publication, many authors and critics have taken apart Gaddis's arguments and analyzed them in detail as part of general evaluations of the work. The most powerful critiques have examined it chapter by chapter to back up general criticisms about the way in which Gaddis constructed his "new Cold Way history."[1] As the historian Melvyn Leffler put it: "I have taken the time to summarize Gaddis's themes at length because he is the preeminent historian of the Cold War, and he is providing a new master narrative to serve as a framework for interpreting the new documents, digesting the new literature, and understanding the framework of international relations for much of the second half of the twentieth century."[2]

The approach that Gaddis took, dealing with aspects of the Cold War individually to further his ambitious aim of arriving at a comprehensive comparative history of the Cold War, meant that critics have had to consider each of his individual arguments one by one if they have wanted to convincingly dismiss the book as a whole. In the end, Leffler concluded that, while it would set the parameters for future study, Gaddis's work focused too much on proving his point (or demonstrating his bias) that the United States' vision of the world was superior to that of the Soviet Union.

NOTES

1 See, for example: Richard Ned Lebow, "We Still Don't Know!" *Diplomatic History* 22, No. 4 (1998): 627–632; and Melvyn P. Leffler, "The Cold War: What Do 'We Now Know'?" *The American Historical Review* 104, No. 2 (1999): 501–524.

2 Leffler, "The Cold War," 506.

ACHIEVEMENT

KEY POINTS

- Although Gaddis has been criticized for his triumphalist* view, claiming that liberal democracy* and capitalism* (the governmental and economical models dominant today in the West) succeeded on account of their inherent superiority to Soviet communism,* he reframed the debate on Cold War* history.

- The influx of new information that became available following the Soviet Union's collapse in 1991 formed the basis for his achievement in *We Now Know*.

- One limitation of the study is that the author could not analyze many documents in their original languages. He depended largely on English sources that reference the most important sources in the Soviet Union, China, and Eastern Europe.

Assessing the Argument

In *We Now Know*, Gaddis's comparative methodology—his way of comparing different pieces of information from different places—proved to be an effective way of looking at new source material from the Soviet Union, Eastern Europe, and the People's Republic of China.

But while most historians were fine with Gaddis's decision to consider the new material and compare it to sources in the United States and allied countries, some argued that his interpretation had problems and merely restated old arguments. (Orthodox interpretations blame the Soviet Union for the Cold War, pointing to the way it tried to "Sovietize" Eastern Europe by imposing Russian cultural models, and to its ambitions to spread communism around the world.)

❝ All of these practices—knowing the outcome, having multiple sources, paying attention to ideas—are decidedly old-fashioned. They are the way history is written most of the time. They suggest not only that the 'old' Cold War history is out of date; it was also an abnormal way of writing history itself. ❞

John Lewis Gaddis, *We Now Know: Rethinking Cold Ware History*

These arguments came in response to Gaddis's claims that the new source material proved that the Soviet Union was responsible for the Cold War, and that, in the end, the resilience of liberal democracy and capitalism stemmed from their superiority to Marxism-Leninism*— the communist ideology of the Soviet Union.

Critics attacked that conclusion as triumphalist* —meaning that the victory of the West in the ideological battle with the Soviet Union colored his analysis in an unhelpful way—and that he held this view even before he wrote the text. But Gaddis predicted this criticism in *We Now Know*, and he tells his readers that triumphalism could be misleading. Although he does not take the point any further, he does manage to shield his argument from that criticism to some extent.

Apart from this point of contention, by presenting his "new Cold War history" in eight clear hypotheses, distilled as one argument in the final chapter, Gaddis reframed the debate on Cold War history and so made a fundamental contribution to the field.

Achievement in Context

Gaddis was a pioneer of a new school of thought on the writing of Cold War history known as post-revisionism.*

Revisionist* Cold War history pointed to the United States' desire for global political dominance, finding America at fault for provoking and perpetuating the tension of the period. But, with the aid of new documentary evidence, Gaddis replaced those arguments with a differently nuanced perspective on how the conflict broke out. As the historian Anders Stephanson* puts it, Gaddis was "less interested, consequently, in the moral implications of the Cold War and who was to blame for it than he was in statecraft and the scope of security claims."[1]

By the time he came to write *We Now Know*, these arguments were also coming under threat—from Gaddis himself. He and other scholars had begun to move away from the accepted schools of thought that had existed before the Cold War ended. The flood of new documents from the Soviet Union and its allies after the end of the Cold War inspired Gaddis to write a comprehensive international history of the conflict—something that had hitherto been impossible, although the work of other historians of the "new Cold War history" certainly influenced him to do so. The American historian Ernest May,* for example, published work arguing that due to different traditions, belief systems, and objectives in world politics, hostility between the United States and Soviet Union was bound to occur following World War II.[2]

Limitations

One limitation of *We Now Know* was that Gaddis was unable to understand many primary documents from Russia, China, and Eastern Europe. In the preface of the text, however, he stressed that the large volume of working papers and monographs in English that referenced the most important of these sources made up for his not being able to analyze them in their original languages. This shows the extent to which the author had thought about potential criticisms of his work and largely pre-empted them.

Gaddis also warned his readers that since he published *We Now Know* right after the Cold War ended, other people would undoubtedly revisit his work as new sources of information became available. Important contributions since, particularly the Norwegian historian Odd Arne Westad's* *The Cold War and the International History of the Twentieth Century* (2010), have argued that we have to see the Cold War as one event in a bigger global history and take non-American and non-Soviet points of view into account. While such critiques have challenged the general thrust of the *We Now Know*, Gaddis is still one of the most important historians on the subject, and he has greatly improved our understanding of Cold War history.

Finally, as with all histories and the historians who write them, *We Now Know* is limited by the constraints of the particular period in which it was written. It was exactly for this reason that Gaddis chose to use the word "now" in the title. And he explicitly says in *We Now Know* that his reason for using it was "to situate this book at a particular point in time, not to claim timelessness for it."[3] The work has become a product of its time in the sense that it represented the first attempt to write a comparative comprehensive international history of the Cold War.

NOTES

1 Anders Stephanson, "Rethinking Cold War History," *Review of International Studies* 24, No. 1 (1998): 119.

2 Ernest May, "The Cold War," in Joseph S. Nye Jr., *The Making of America's Soviet Policy* (New Haven: Yale University Press, 1984), 209–230.

3 John Lewis Gaddis, *We Now Know: Rethinking Cold War History* (Oxford: Clarendon Press, 1997), viii.

PLACE IN THE AUTHOR'S WORK

KEY POINTS

- John Lewis Gaddis published We Now Know at the mid-point of his academic career. He was already a well known scholar of the Cold War* and international history more broadly.

- *We Now Know* moved beyond Gaddis's previous influential work on the school of historical analysis known as post-revisionism.*

- Gaddis's body of work is an important reference point in the field of history and has served as a foundation for further scholarship and debate.

Positioning

When John Lewis Gaddis published *We Now Know: Rethinking Cold War History*, he was already a historian of repute. He had worked as a researcher and instructor at Ohio University since 1969, and he had held the title of Distinguished Professor there since 1983. He had also been a visiting professor of strategy at the Naval War College, a Harold Vyvyan Harmsworth Visiting Professor of American History at Oxford University and a Whitney Shepardson Fellow at the Council on Foreign Relations.[1] He was also the author of four books, the most famous of which was *Strategies of Containment* (1982), a work that focused on the US strategy of containment,* a diplomatic and military strategy designed to impede Soviet imperialism.*

Gaddis wrote *We Now Know* at the mid-point of his academic career and immediately after the end of the Cold War. His first studies were published in the early 1970s[2] while relations between the United States and the Soviet Union were still tense. During this period, the

❝ This volume is likely to set the parameters for a whole new generation of scholarship. No historian is better known for his work on the Cold War. ❞

Melvyn Leffler,* "Review Essay: The Cold War: What do 'We Now Know'?"

debate on the subject in historiographical* terms (that is, in approaches to writing history) concerned the struggle between orthodox* historians, who held opinions developed during the Cold War, and revisionist* historians, who held contrary opinions formed at the end of the period and immediately following it. Following the collapse of the Soviet Union, Gaddis waded into the debate by reframing it entirely and establishing a post-revisionist* school of thought.

Integration

Gaddis's 1982 article, "The Emerging Post-Revisionist Synthesis on the Origins of the Cold War,"[3] quickly became highly influential, helping him become one of the most important Cold War thinkers of his generation. By the time he came to write *We Now Know*, he had become "the one historian even pundits read."[4] But Gaddis was prepared to risk this reputation with *We Now Know*, as it meant a complete departure from his work on post-revisionism in favor of a comparative approach: "new Cold War history." It was a bold move, but it paid off. The book was met with widespread critical acclaim and set the tone for further scholarship.

Gaddis continues to show an open mind. When he published *We Now Know* in 1997, he was already aware that his ideas would continue to develop and change in the future; the phrase "we now know" designated what was known at the particular point in time at which the book had been published. In his words: "I reserve the right in the light of new evidence to change my mind, just as this volume revises much of what I have previously thought and argued."[5]

Indeed, the most recent book he has written on the Cold War, a 2005 overview of the entire conflict, further refined and developed the arguments that he first made in *We Now Know*, as well as introduced them to a much wider general audience. In *The Cold War*, he argues that, given the fact that both sides' access to nuclear weapons had neutralized military conflict, the most important element of the Cold War was the power of ideas. Ultimately, he claims that liberal democracy* and capitalism* provided hope to citizens while Soviet communism did not. This latter work won Gaddis the prestigious Harry S. Truman book prize.

Although *We Now Know* proved very important to the study of Cold War history when it was first published, it has, if anything, only become even more influential.

Significance

The appearance of Gaddis's comprehensive study of the international history of the Cold War in 1997 was well timed. In a post–Cold War world, many readers were looking for a book that could explain the event as history, not current affairs. As a result, Gaddis became the prominent authority on the "new Cold War history." The fact that *We Now Know* remains a seminal text for students of the Cold War today, despite the huge influx of new documents that have been released since its publication, shows how important it still is, even though its author did not expect it to be timeless.

As well as winning awards and appreciation for his studies of the Cold War as an international history, Gaddis has also been a highly influential historian of American grand strategy*—that is, the US's policy of using every means available to achieve its aims. His early work on that and the theory and practice of containment*—the American policy of trying to limit the spread of communism—was also a critical success. Gaddis continued to work on the subject of containment over the years until he eventually produced the official biography of George F. Kennan,* the American statesman and principal architect of containment, for which Gaddis was awarded a prestigious Pulitzer Prize.

Considering all this, it is clear that Gaddis has had an outstanding academic career. We can expect his contributions to the field of Cold War history to remain influential, and controversial, for decades to come. His body of work is essential reading for any scholar interested in the international history of the period.

NOTES

1   John Lewis Gaddis, *What We Now Know: Rethinking Cold War History* (Oxford, Clarendon Press, 1997), vii–ix.

2   John Lewis Gaddis, *The United States and the Origins of the Cold War, 1941–1947* (New York: Colombia University Press, 1972).

3   John Lewis Gaddis, "The Emerging Post-Revisionist Synthesis on the Origins of the Cold War," *Diplomatic History 7*, No. 3 (1983): 131–48.

4   Anders Stephanson, "Rethinking Cold War History," *Review of International Studies* 24, No. 1 (1998): 119.

5   John Lewis Gaddis, *Now Know: Rethinking Cold War History* (Oxford: Clarendon Press, 1997), viii.

SECTION 3
IMPACT

THE FIRST RESPONSES

KEY POINTS

- Gaddis's critics have claimed that, rather than focusing on the essence of the Cold War,* he concentrated too much on showing that the political, economic, and social structures of the US doctrine were superior to those of the Soviet Union.

- Although the author has not engaged in direct debate with his critics, he has modified his arguments in response to their criticisms in subsequent works on Cold War history.

- Scholars today have moved beyond Gaddis's thesis by attempting to situate the Cold War within a longer history, rather than analyzing it as a single event.

Criticism

John Lewis Gaddis's *We Now Know* was strongly criticized when it was first published. Melvyn Leffler,* another prominent Cold War historian, was one of the most vocal critics of the book. He argued that, although Gaddis had been a pioneer of the post-revisionist* school of historical analysis, he was more concerned with placing the blame for the Cold War on the Soviet Union than on understanding how it came about. In this regard, he claims that the text reasserted many of the orthodox* arguments on how the conflict began.

The political scientist Irene Gendzier* put similar concerns in more blunt terms by saying that the work was "above all a contribution to the retraditionalization of Cold War history in which the apologetic treatment of US policy mutes much of what we now know from the public record."[1] By this, she meant that Gaddis's analysis returned to a traditional interpretation of the historical facts.

> 66 One empire arose, therefore, by invitation, the other by imposition. *Europeans* made this distinction, very much as they had done during the war when they welcomed armies liberating them from the west but feared those that came from the east. They did so because they saw clearly at the time—even if a subsequent generation would not always see—how different American and Soviet empires were likely to be. It is true that the *extent* of the American empire quickly exceeded that of its Soviet counterpart, but this was because *resistance* to expanding American influence was never as great. 99
>
> John Lewis Gaddis, *We Now Know: Rethinking Cold War History*

Leffler made further criticisms. He argued that Gaddis had come to the firm conclusion that the Cold War was unavoidable while Joseph Stalin* was in charge of the Soviet Union "without closely examining Stalin's actions."[2] Richard Lebow agreed, and pointed out what he called "an unresolved ambiguity in the book about the Cold War and Stalin's relation to it."[3] According to Leffler, the book was worryingly full of "the triumphalism* that runs through our contemporary culture."[4] He also argued that the neat conclusions it made ran the risk of becoming outdated—that, as time passed, the arguments that Gaddis put forth in *We Now Know* would start to seem nothing more than products of the immediate post-Cold War era. He warned Gaddis: "In writing about the Cold War after the Cold War, we should not confuse its ending with its origins and evolution."[5]

Responses

Many historians said that the work actually contained very little that was new—that it was just a rounding up of old arguments. Although some of those criticisms were persuasive, it would have been hard for Gaddis to accept them all without fundamentally undermining his methods and conclusions.

Nevertheless, we can see evidence in Gaddis's more recent writing that developments in Cold War historiography* since *We Now Know* was published have changed the way he thinks. This is clear in his most recent book on the topic, *The Cold War*, published in 2005, which covers the whole conflict in a much more succinct manner than *We Now Know*. Discussing the Cold War in that book's preface, Gaddis accepts that: "Any attempt to reduce the history of it to the role of great forces, great powers, or great leaders would fail to do it justice. Any effort to capture it within a simple chronological narrative could only produce mush."[6]

Although Gaddis has not been involved in direct debate since he published the latter work, he seems to have accepted the consensus among historians that the Cold War was too large an event to summarize in any single-volume history, no matter how ambitious or talented the historian. He also seems to have accepted criticisms that the war was fought on many fronts, and other participants—not merely the United States and the Soviet Union—influenced its outcome.

Conflict and Consensus

We Now Know is still very relevant to historians of the Cold War, although perhaps not in the way in which Gaddis expected or intended when he wrote it.

The text remains an influential study of the "new Cold War history" that began immediately as the period ended, when a huge flood of new documentary evidence became available, allowing a reinterpretation of previously accepted historical facts. It was one of the first texts to try to rethink Cold War history in a comprehensive way through the comparison of documents from different sources, and it still represents an important milestone in the evolution of the historiography. Since its publication, however, Cold War historians have moved away from the master narrative approach—telling the whole story in one big overview—towards a more nuanced and varied understanding of the Cold War that attempts to position it as one event within a much wider historical context.

In *We Now Know*, Gaddis helped start this movement by suggesting that the "new Cold War history" needed to leave the old polarized arguments behind and treat the Cold War as a particular episode instead of a permanent condition. Reviewers of the book agreed. Richard Lebow,* a well known scholar of international relations, argued that "'new' history also needs new questions. Let us leave behind the question of who started the Cold War—still a central theme of this book—and pose more interesting, important, and productive questions that will provide insight into the past the present."[7]

NOTES

1   Irene L. Gendzier, "The Saints Come Marching In: A Response to John Lewis Gaddis," in *After the Fall: 1989 and the Future of Freedom*, ed. George N. Katsiaficas (London: Routledge, 2001), 162.

2   Melvyn P. Leffler, "The Cold War: What Do 'We Now Know'?" *The American Historical Review* 104, No. 2 (1999): 503.

3   Richard Ned Lebow, "We Still Don't Know!" *Diplomatic History* 22, No. 4 (1998): 628.

4   Leffler, "The Cold War," 523.

5   Leffler, "The Cold War," 524.

6   John Lewis Gaddis, *The Cold War* (London: Allen Lane, 2005), ix.

7   Lebow, "We Still Don't Know!," 632.

THE EVOLVING DEBATE

KEY POINTS

- Other historians used Gaddis's method of analysis in *We Now Know* to reach different conclusions.
- Gaddis was criticized for questioning his earlier analysis.
- Historians today focus more on the role of ideas, ideologies, and cultures than on the grand strategy* perspectives that Gaddis adopted.

Uses and Problems

John Lewis Gaddis recognized the complexity of the historical forces that shaped the Cold War in *We Now Know.* But this complexity meant that historians reacted to *We Now Know* in interesting and unpredictable ways. Although the book challenged the work of historians who had once supported him, it also built bridges between Gaddis and some of his more passionate critics.

As the debate has unfolded, scholars have conducted historical studies on a wide range of topics that all deal, in some way or another, with the Cold War. Explorations of themes as varied as ideas, values, language, culture, race, gender, geopolitics, economics, and domestic political culture, to name but a few, have all appeared since Gaddis published *We Now Know.*[1] That has affected the power and validity of many of the conclusions he made in the text for the precise reason that he anticipated when writing the book: today, "we now know" much more.

But the text is still relevant to students because: 1) it is an accessible and well-written overview of some of the key events of the early Cold

> 66 What is there new to say about the old question of responsibility for the Cold War? Who actually started it? Could it have been averted? Here I think the 'new' Cold War history is bringing us back to an old answer: that *as long as Stalin was running the Soviet Union a cold war was unavoidable.* 99
>
> John Lewis Gaddis, *We Now Know: Rethinking Cold War History*

War, and 2) it is the first comprehensive comparative account of that event. It remains a necessary text for anyone trying to understand the parameters of the current debate around Cold War history.

Schools of Thought

Gaddis's methodology in *We Now Know* challenged the post-revisionist* school of Cold War historians—a surprise to many, as Gaddis had previously been at the forefront of the movement. During the latter years of the Cold War, he and his close supporters had argued in favor of a realistic explanation for the outbreak of the Cold War—that it was basically all about national interests, grand strategy,* and great power politics (that is, a political strategy based on deliberate aggression and threat) and that ideology, ideas, and beliefs were not important. But with access to new documents from the Soviet Union, China, and Eastern Europe, Gaddis fundamentally revised his views and returned to some orthodox* arguments about how the Cold War began.

For example, he placed greater emphasis on the role of Stalin* and his ideological compulsions in the outbreak of the Cold War. That meant that historians like the Norwegian historian Geir Lundestad,* who had once passionately supported his post-revisionist stance, now began to oppose him. Lundestad argued that Gaddis was "being far too critical of his own earlier views and that his new views represent a dangerous return to the orthodox school of interpretation."[2]

In contrast, historians who were once bitterly opposed to Gaddis's interpretation of the Cold War now seemed to share his methodological approach. The historian Anders Stephanson,* for example, who argued that American ideology was the most important contributing factor to the outbreak of the Cold War, had employed a similar methodology to the one that Gaddis used in *We Now Know*. The only difference was that Stephanson came to the exact opposite conclusion about which country's ideology had provoked the Cold War.

In Current Scholarship

Current supporters of the methodological approach to studying the history of the Cold War employed in *We Now Know* still support its central premise that the "new Cold War history" must be based on archival material and must be comparative. Historians now tend to focus more on the part played by ideas, ideologies, and cultures than grand strategy*—an analysis that Gaddis supported.

Some scholars, such as the Cold War historian Odd Arne Westad, have emphasized concepts. For him, "[the] belief that each group involved in the conflict had sets of concepts or ideas which defined and constituted them" is an important feature of historical interpretation. "Often (though not exclusively) focusing on ideologies and patterns of thought, conceptualist historians tend to see a much wider variety of human agendas and processes of change intermingled in the conflict we now call the Cold War," according to Westad.[3]

In the intellectual world of the new generation of Cold War historians, *We Now Know* provides historians with a methodological framework from which to write new international histories of the Cold War. It continues to be an important starting point for Cold War studies.

Supporters of this approach to Cold War history, and international history in general, are very influential today. These historians—

working with the most recently opened archives—are now writing histories of the Cold War from novel points of view, exploring new transnational, cultural, geopolitical and societal sides to the conflict.

"Understanding the place of the Cold War within the overall history of the twentieth century is very much about understanding global processes of change,"[4] writes Westad. A new generation of historians, inspired by the determination of Gaddis in *We Now Know* to explore the Cold War in new and exciting ways, has followed his lead in order to explain the conflict in extraordinary detail to the next generation of Cold War scholars.

NOTES

1 Melvyn P. Leffler, "The Cold War: What Do 'We Now Know'?" *The American Historical Review* 104 (1999) 2: 501–2.

2 Odd Arne Westad, "Introduction: Reviewing the Cold War," in *Reviewing the Cold War: Approaches, Interpretations, Theory*, ed. Odd Arne Westad (London: Frank Cass, 2000), 5.

3 Odd Arne Westad, "The Cold War and the International History of the Twentieth Century," in *The Cambridge History of the Cold War*, Vol. 1, ed. Melvyn P. Leffler and Odd Arne Westad (Cambridge: Cambridge University Press, 2010), 6.

4 Westad, "The Cold War," 17.

MODULE 11
IMPACT AND INFLUENCE TODAY

KEY POINTS

- While scholars agree that the Cold War* was too vast and complicated an event for one master narrative to effectively summarize it, *We Now Know* remains an important reference point in Cold War studies.

- However, since history evolves, and debate has progressed, the text is no longer central to current debate.

- Today, the Cold War is a historical event and not a matter of current affairs, so historians seek to understand it within a longer period of history rather than analyzing it as a single development.

Position

In the decade and a half since John Lewis Gaddis published *We Now Know*, a new generation of Cold War historians has revisited and refined its ideas. Although Gaddis confessed in his concluding remarks that the text was unlikely to remain definitive as time went on, he did intend for it to provide readers with the first comprehensive comparative international history of the Cold War.

After publication, critics attacked this idea as unrealistic—they thought that the Cold War was simply too vast and complicated an event to be summed up properly in one master narrative. Historians wanted to move away from what they thought were simplistic questions on who started the Cold War in order to explore the event in the broader context of the international history of the twentieth century.

As Odd Arne Westad put it in a recent essay: "We need to place the Cold War in the larger context of chronological time and geographical

66 Limited access to Soviet and Chinese archives, a flood of documents from Eastern Europe, and the general willingness of former Soviet-bloc officials to talk about the past have stimulated an exciting rethinking and rewriting of postwar history. *We Now Know* exploits this archival research and the publications based on it to reassess some of the major controversies surrounding the first fifteen years of the Cold War. 99

Richard Ned Lebow,* "We Still Don't Know!"

space within the web that ties the never-ending threads of history together ... We need to indicate how Cold War conflicts connect to broader trends in social economic and intellectual history as well as to the political and military developments of the longer term of which it forms a part."[1]

Interaction

We Now Know still serves a purpose as an exceptionally well-written and detailed general international history of the first third of the Cold War. It provides new students of that conflict with a useful introduction to the most important events of that early period, as well as an important understanding of the central tenets of the "new Cold War history" as Gaddis defined it. Although the debate over the historical understanding of the Cold War has moved beyond that of great-power interactions and grand strategy* towards a more nuanced and contextualized understanding of it as simply one aspect of the international history of the twentieth century as a whole,[2] *We Now Know* remains influential—even if it is no longer challenging or transforming existing ideas about Cold War history.

We Now Know also continues to act as the standard bearer for a method of historical analysis that uses documentary evidence from the former Soviet Union and its allies to restate traditional arguments on who was to blame for the Cold War. But as the mainstream of Cold War history has moved away from this debate, this argument is less relevant.

The Continuing Debate

We Now Know represents an important introduction to the current intellectual debate on the historical understanding of the Cold War, even if its central arguments have since been developed and refined by other historians, and even by the author himself. Ideas about the Cold War have significantly changed since Gaddis wrote *We Now Know.* At that time, when new documentary evidence was still only just coming to light from the former Soviet Union, its Eastern European allies, and the People's Republic of China, historians, with Gaddis at the forefront, were keen to pass judgment on a Cold War that had only just ended. In *We Now Know*, Gaddis wanted to produce the first comparative international history of the Cold War.

But the debate has now moved on, and the passage of time has brought historical detachment from it. As Gaddis has acknowledged in a more recent history of the conflict, young scholars today do not even remember when the Cold War was a current phenomenon, rather than a historical one.

Now that the Cold War has become simply another historical event, historians have less political motivation to analyze it from the point of view of a clash of ideological superpowers, as orthodox* and revisionist* historians commonly did before its end in 1991. Historians now want to understand the Cold War in the larger context of international history and to explore how it interacted with factors such as race, culture, language, gender, media, and many other criteria. This process culminated in the publication in 2010 of the exhaustive and authoritative *Cambridge History of the Cold War.*[3] This three-volume work of 2,000 pages explored a huge range of topics that relate in some way or another to the international history of the Cold War. But even so, its editor stressed that no history of the Cold War could be, or ever should be, considered the last word.[4]

Gaddis contributed to this study himself by writing an essay on grand strategies of the Cold War.[5] As one part of a much more detailed anthology of work, this essay demonstrated Gaddis's understanding that Cold War history has changed.

NOTES

1   Odd Arne Westad, "The Cold War and the International History of the Twentieth Century," in *The Cambridge History of the Cold War*, Vol 1, ed. Melvyn P. Leffler and Odd Arne Westad (Cambridge: Cambridge University Press, 2010), 6.

2   Westad, "The Cold War and the International History of the Twentieth Century," 2.

3   Melvyn P. Leffler and Odd Arne Westad, eds., *The Cambridge History of the Cold War* (Cambridge: Cambridge University Press, 2010).

4   Westad, "The Cold War and the International History of the Twentieth Century," 2.

5   John Lewis Gaddis, "Grand strategies in the Cold War," in *The Cambridge History of the Cold War*, Vol. 2, eds. Melvyn P. Leffler and Odd Arne Westad (Cambridge: Cambridge University Press, 2010), 1–21.

WHERE NEXT?

KEY POINTS

- The importance of *We Now Know* lies in the fact that it was the first study after the Cold War* ended to compare new sources.
- The study of the Cold War is no longer exclusively focused on political and diplomatic history. It is seen as an event within a longer period of history that can be examined within different disciplines.
- Today, scholars have moved beyond a bipolar focus to understand the role of other countries in the Cold War, given that it was a globally significant event.

Potential

John Lewis Gaddis's *We Now Know* has become the standard text of "new Cold War history."

With more access to a much wider range of archives, and by focusing on a much greater diversity of context, recent studies may have overtaken the text's central ideas. But that does not mean that *We Now Know* is irrelevant today. In the same way that any Cold War scholar still needs to be familiar with orthodox* and revisionist* "Cold War histories," Gaddis's work will always be important for understanding the approach to Cold War history that he helped to develop.

Even if the debate about the Cold War has become more nuanced, international, and diversified than was possible when Gaddis wrote *We Now Know*, nothing can change the fact that the book broke new ground when it first appeared. It also helped put Cold War historians

> 66 Finally, how will the Cold War look a hundred years hence? Not as it does today, it seems safe enough to say, just as the Cold War we now know looks different from the one we knew, or thought we knew, while it was going on. It ought to humble historians to recognize how much their views of the past—any past, no matter how distant—reflect the particular present in which they find themselves. We are all, in this sense, *temporal* parochials. There follows, then, one last hypothesis: *"new" Cold War historians should retain the capacity to be surprised.* 99
>
> John Lewis Gaddis, *We Now Know: Rethinking Cold War History*

on the path to writing the type of Cold War history that has become commonplace. For these reasons, there is no doubt that it will continue to be considered a seminal text for students of Cold War history.

Future Directions

Since the publication of *We Now Know*, historians have increasingly treated the Cold War as a global phenomenon. Cold War research now crosses a variety of disciplines and, along with the access to new archives, that has helped redefine the meaning of the conflict. Current study of the Cold War no longer focuses on traditional political and diplomatic history alone. Instead it includes transnational, social, and cultural history, among many other elements. Within this context, it is hard to imagine future historiographical* debates on the Cold War centering on the arguments in *We Now Know*. The field of reference of the "new Cold War" history has expanded too far beyond the confines of that text.

But, as the first work of "new Cold War history" to consider the new source material and produce a comparative international history of the period not long after it ended, *We Now Know* will continue to be relevant to Cold War scholars—at least as an introduction to the subject. It is probable that, like many recent accounts of the Cold War, new historians will continue to develop Gaddis's original ideas. Today, many studies are trying to take a wider view of this topic in terms of theme and geography than Gaddis was able to provide. They have moved their focus away from the bipolar contest between the United States and the Soviet Union towards "globalizing" Cold War concepts, giving greater attention to other regions and countries. In short, they have put the Cold War in context as part of the international history of the twentieth century.[1]

Summary

We Now Know still deserves special attention from all historians and students of the history of the Cold War. Although the debate has moved on significantly since its publication, the book remains a seminal study of the origins of the Cold War. Gaddis's accessible writing style, his talented working of source material from across the ideological divide, and his ability to piece together complicated and diverse events during the early Cold War produced a persuasive synthesis. This is a study of enduring relevance both to the casual reader and the serious historian.

Since the publication of *We Now* Know, Gaddis has maintained his reputation as one of the world's most prominent Cold War historians. His arguments, ideas, and thoughts on the subject are taken seriously and debated by some of the most reputed scholars in this field. *The Cold War*, his latest work on the topic, is a concise but comprehensive overview of the entire conflict and was awarded the Harry S. Truman book prize in 2006. Critics have also praised his official biography of the famous "cold warrior"[2] George F. Kennan,* which received a Pulitzer Prize in 2012.[3] *We Now Know* laid the foundations for this success; Gaddis has revised his method and interpretation in later works.

The impact *We Now Know* had when it first appeared was significant in terms of the wide audience it reached, the plaudits it received, and in the range of criticism it attracted. An ambitious work on a topic that is always controversial was bound to attract praise and criticism in equal measure.

But despite the arguments of its detractors, no one could deny that Gaddis had produced a study that was unique at the time. The end of the Cold War allowed him to conduct the first, comprehensive, comparative international history of the conflict. No matter how much the "new Cold War history" evolved over the coming years and decades, it is indisputable that Gaddis was the first to define that school of thought and that he blazed a trail for other historians to follow.

NOTES

1 Odd Arne Westad, "The Cold War and the International History of the Twentieth Century," in *The Cambridge History of the Cold War*, Vol. 1, eds. Melvyn P. Leffler and Odd Arne Westad (Cambridge: Cambridge University Press, 2010), 2.

2 A person involved in the development and execution of American or Soviet policy during the Cold War.

3 John Lewis Gaddis, *George F. Kennan: An American Life* (New York: The Penguin Press, 2011).

GLOSSARY

GLOSSARY OF TERMS

Anarchy: commonly, a state of disorder due to absence of authority; in international relations theory, the absence of a world government.

Balance of Power: in international relations theory, this is a situation where different nations counter each other's influence to create stability. Realists propose this as a means of dealing with anarchy* (the absence of a world government).

Capitalism: an economic system that emphasizes the private ownership of the means of production. "The means of production" refers to those things that are necessary for the production of goods— such as land, natural resources, and technology.

Chinese Civil War: a protracted conflict in China (1927–36 and 1946–50) between the nationalist forces of the Republic of China (ROC) and forces of the Communist Party of China, eventually resulting in the establishment of the People's Republic of China.

Cold War: hostility between the United States and its allies and the Soviet Union and its allies that began after the end of World War II and continued until the fall of the Berlin Wall and the collapse of the Soviet Union.

Collective security: a system by which international peace and security is maintained by an association of nations.

Communism: a political ideology that relies on the state ownership of the means of production, the collectivization of labor, and the abolition of social class. It was the ideology of the Soviet Union (1917–91).

Containment: A policy designed by the American diplomat George F. Kennan* and the United States government to prevent perceived efforts by the Soviet Union to spread communism* to other foreign countries.

Cuban Missile Crisis: a political and military crisis in 1962 involving the United States, the Soviet Union, and Cuba. It began after the American government discovered that the Soviet Union was placing nuclear missiles on Cuban territory.

Eastern Bloc: a term used by the United States and its allies during the Cold War★ to refer to the Soviet Union and its allies.

Grand Strategy: the deliberate use of all instruments of power at the disposal of a nation, or an alliance of nations, to attain a defined policy goal.

Historiography: a term meaning either the study of the methodology of writing history or the body of historical work that exists on a specific topic.

Imperialism: the extension of a nation's influence by territorial acquisition or by the establishment of political and economic dominance over other nations.

Korean War: a war between 1950 and 1953 between the communist Democratic People's Republic of Korea (DPRK) and the Republic of Korea (ROK) to unite the Korean peninsula under one government. It is often considered to have been not only a civil war but also a proxy war between the superpowers in the Cold War, who sponsored different sides of the conflict.

Liberal Democracy: a political system that emphasizes human and civil rights, regular and free elections between competing political parties, and adherence to the rule of law.

Marxism-Leninism: a political ideology that combines a Marxist analysis of capitalism—socialist concepts developed by the political philosopher and economist Karl Marx (1818–83) and the industrialist Friedrich Engels (1820–1895)—with Leninism (theories of revolutionary action developed by Vladimir Lenin (1870–1924), the first leader of the Soviet Union).

Orthodox: a scholarly approach that holds the Soviet Union responsible for the Cold War because of its "Sovietization" of Eastern Europe (that is, the imposition of a governmental and cultural model developed in Russia) and ambitions to spread communism around the world.

Post-Revisionism: the practice of replacing old revisionist or orthodox arguments about the origins of the Cold War with interpretations stressing the importance on geopolitics and power balances.

Revisionism: an interpretation of events that places greater responsibility for the Cold War* on the United States by emphasizing its imperialist tendencies and ambitions to dominate global affairs.

Russian Revolution: a collective term for a series of revolutionary uprisings in Imperial Russia that deposed the ruling Tsar Nicholas II and ultimately led to the creation in 1917 of a Russian socialist state ruled by communists.

Third World: a term commonly used for the underdeveloped and developing countries of Asia, Africa, and Latin America.

Triumphalism: usually, an excessive glee in triumph; triumphalism might color historical analysis by preventing a fully objective analysis.

Soviet Bloc: the communist nations that were closely allied with the Soviet Union during the Cold War.

Stalinism: the ideology of Joseph Stalin—an authoritarian, centralized form of communism.

Woodrow Wilson Center: an institution in the United States, based in Washington, concerned with research and communication in global affairs.

World War I (1914–18): a global conflict fought between the Central Powers (Germany, Austria-Hungary, and the Ottoman Empire) and the victorious Allied Powers (Britain, France, Russia and, after 1917, the United States). More than 16 million people died as a result of the war.

World War II (1939–1945): also known as the Second World War, the most widespread military conflict in history, resulting in more than 50 million casualties. While the conflict began with Germany's invasion of Poland in 1939, it soon involved all of the major world powers, which gradually formed two military alliances and were eventually joined by a great number of the world's nations.

PEOPLE MENTIONED IN THE TEXT

Neal Ascherson (b. 1932) is a well-known Scottish journalist and writer. He worked for the *Observer*, among other important press outlets.

Fidel Castro (b. 1926) is a Cuban politician and revolutionary. He was prime minister of Cuba from 1959 to 1976 and president of the country from 1976 to 2008.

Jian Chen is Distinguished Global Network Professor of History at New York University, Shanghai. He is a leading scholar on the Cold War,* modern Chinese History, and the history of Chinese-American relations.

Robert Divine is George W. Littlefield Professor Emeritus of History. He was John Lewis Gaddis's PhD advisor.

Irene Gendzier is a professor of political science at Boston University.

Louis Halle (1910–88) was a distinguished scholar of international studies. He was also a member of the policy planning staff at the US Department of State during the Korean and Vietnam Wars.

David Hendrickson is Robert J. Fox Distinguished Service Professor of Political Science at Colorado College. He has published several important works, including *Peace Pact: The Lost World of the American Founding* (2003).

Eric Hobsbawm (1917–2002) was a well-known British Marxist historian. He wrote several seminal works, including *The Age of Revolution* (1962), *The Age of Capital* (1975), and *The Age of Empire* (1987).

Kim Il-Sung (1912–94) was the leader of North Korea from 1948 until his death in 1994.

George F. Kennan (1904–2005) was an American historian and diplomat. He was a key figure during the Cold War.

John F. Kennedy (1917–63) was president of the United States from 1961 until his assassination in 1963. He was president during the Cuban Missile Crisis.

Nikita Khrushchev (1894–1971) was the leader of the Soviet Union from 1956 to 1964. He was president during the Cuban Missile Crisis.

Richard Ned Lebow is a professor emeritus at Dartmouth College and a professor of international political theory at King's College London. He is an expert on the Cold War and international relations more broadly.

Melvyn Leffler is Edward Stettinius Professor of History at the University of Virginia. He is the author of several important works, including *For the Soul of Mankind: the United States, the Soviet Union, and the Cold War* (2008).

Howard H. Lentner (1932–2014) was a professor emeritus and chair of the political science department at Baruch College. He was an expert on international relations and foreign policy.

Geir Lundestad (b. 1945) is a Norwegian historian and former director of the Norwegian Nobel Institute. He is the author of several important works, including *International Relations Since the End of the Cold War: New and Old Dimensions in International Relations* (2013).

Ernest May (1928–2009) was a renowned American historian of international relations. He was a professor at Harvard University for 55 years and the author of 14 books.

Constantine Pleshakov is currently a visiting professor of international relations at Mount Holyoke College in Massachusetts, USA. Previously, he was director of the geopolitics department at the Institute of US and Canada Studies at the Russian Academy of Sciences from 1986 to 1996.

Joseph Stalin (1878–1953) was the leader of the Soviet Union from 1922 until his death in 1953.

Anders Stephanson is Andrew and Virginia Rudd Family Foundation Professor of History. He is the author of several important works, including *Kennan and the Art of Foreign Policy* (1989).

William Stueck is Distinguished Research Professor of History at the University of Georgia. He is an expert on the Korean War* and US–Korean relations.

Odd Arne Wested is a Norwegian historian and a specialist in Cold War history and international affairs. He is a professor of international history at the London School of Economics and Political Science. He was the co-editor of *The Cambridge History of the Cold War.*

Mao Zedong (1893–1976) was a Chinese communist revolutionary and the founding father of the People's Republic of China.

Vladislav Zubok is a professor of international history at the London School of Economics and Political Science. He is the author of several important works, including *A Failed Empire: the Soviet Union in the Cold War from Stalin to Gorbachev* (2007).

WORKS CITED

WORKS CITED

Ascherson, Neal. "Khrushchev's Secret." *London Review of Books* 19, No. 20. (1997): 26–8.

Chen, Jian. *China's Road to the Korean War: The Making of the Sino-American Confrontation*. New York: Columbia University Press, 1994.

Gaddis, John Lewis. *George F. Kennan: An American Life*. New York: The Penguin Press, 2011.

____. *Strategies of Containment: A Critical Appraisal of Postwar American National Security Policy*. New York: Oxford University Press, 1982.

____. *The Cold War*. London: Allen Lane, 2005.

____. *The United States and the Origins of the Cold War, 1941–1947*. New York: Colombia University Press, 1972.

____. *We Now Know: Rethinking Cold War History*. Oxford: Clarendon Press, 1997.

____. "A Grand Strategy of Transformation." *Foreign Policy* 133 (2002): 50–57.

____. "Grand Strategies in the Cold War." In *The Cambridge History of the Cold War, Volume 2: Crises and Détente*, edited by Melvyn P. Leffler and Odd Arne Westad. Cambridge: Cambridge University Press, 2010.

____. "Grand Strategy in the Second Term." *Foreign Affairs* 84 (2005) 1: 2-15.

____. "The Emerging Post-Revisionist Synthesis on the Origins of the Cold War." *Diplomatic History* 7, No. 3 (1983): 131–48.

Gendzier, Irene L. "The Saints Come Marching In: A Response to John Lewis Gaddis." In *After the Fall: 1989 and the Future of Freedom*, edited by George N. Katsiaficas. London: Routledge, 2001.

Halle, Louis. *The Cold War As History*. New York: Harper and Row, 1967.

Hendrickson, David. "Review: *We Now Know: Rethinking Cold War History*." *Foreign Affairs* (July–August 1997).

Hobsbawm, Eric. *The Age of Extremes: A History of the World, 1914–1991*. New York: Pantheon, 1994.

Judt, Tony. "A Story Still To Be Told." The *New York Review of Books*, March 23, 2006.

Lebow, Richard Ned, "We Still Don't Know!" *Diplomatic History* 22, No. 4 (1998): 627–32.

Leffler, Melvyn P. *The Specter of Communism: The United States and the Origins of the Cold War, 1917–1953*. New York: Hill & Wang, 1994.

____. "The Cold War: What Do 'We Now Know'?" *The American Historical Review* 104, No. 2 (1999): 501–24.

Leffler, Melvyn P and Odd Arne Westad. *The Cambridge History of the Cold War*. Cambridge: Cambridge University Press, 2010.

Lentner, Howard H. "New Cold War History: A Review of *We Now Know: Rethinking Cold War History*." *H-Teachpol* (February, 1998).

Lundestad, Geir. "Empire by Invitation? The United States and Western Europe, 1945–1952." *Journal of Peace Research* 23, No. 3 (1986): 263–77.

May, Ernest. "The Cold War." In *The Making of America's Soviet Policy*, edited by Joseph S. Nye Jr. New Haven: Yale University Press, 1984.

Stephanson, Anders. "Rethinking Cold War History." *Review of International Studies* 24, No. 1 (1998): 119–24.

Stueck, William. *The Korean War: An International History*. Princeton: Princeton University Press, 1995.

Westad, Odd Arne. *Cold War and Revolution: Soviet-American Rivalry and the Origins of the Chinese Civil War, 1944–1946*. New York: Columbia University Press, 1993.

____. "Bibliographical Essay: The Cold War and the International History of the Twentieth Century." In *The Cambridge History of the Cold War, Volume 1: Origins*, edited by Melvyn P. Leffler and Odd Arne Westad. Cambridge: Cambridge University Press, 2010.

____. "Introduction: Reviewing the Cold War." In *Reviewing the Cold War: Approaches, Interpretations, Theory*, edited by Odd Arne Westad. London: Frank Cass, 2000.

____. "The Cold War and the International History of the Twentieth Century." In *The Cambridge History of the Cold War, Volume 1: Origins*, edited by Melvyn P. Leffler and Odd Arne Westad. Cambridge: Cambridge University Press, 2010.

Zhang, Shu Guang. *Deterrence and Strategic Culture: Chinese-American Confrontations, 1949–1958*. Ithaca: Cornell University Press, 1992.

____. *Mao's Military Romanticism: China and the Korean War, 1950–1953*. Lawrence: University Press of Kansas, 1995.

Zubok, Vladislav and Constantine Pleshakov. *Inside the Kremlin's Cold War: From Stalin to Khrushchev*. Cambridge, MA: Harvard University Press, 1996.

THE MACAT LIBRARY
BY DISCIPLINE

AFRICANA STUDIES

Chinua Achebe's *An Image of Africa: Racism in Conrad's Heart of Darkness*
W. E. B. Du Bois's *The Souls of Black Folk*
Zora Neale Huston's *Characteristics of Negro Expression*
Martin Luther King Jr's *Why We Can't Wait*
Toni Morrison's *Playing in the Dark: Whiteness in the American Literary Imagination*

ANTHROPOLOGY

Arjun Appadurai's *Modernity at Large: Cultural Dimensions of Globalisation*
Philippe Ariès's *Centuries of Childhood*
Franz Boas's *Race, Language and Culture*
Kim Chan & Renée Mauborgne's *Blue Ocean Strategy*
Jared Diamond's *Guns, Germs & Steel: the Fate of Human Societies*
Jared Diamond's *Collapse: How Societies Choose to Fail or Survive*
E. E. Evans-Pritchard's *Witchcraft, Oracles and Magic Among the Azande*
James Ferguson's *The Anti-Politics Machine*
Clifford Geertz's *The Interpretation of Cultures*
David Graeber's *Debt: the First 5000 Years*
Karen Ho's *Liquidated: An Ethnography of Wall Street*
Geert Hofstede's *Culture's Consequences: Comparing Values, Behaviors, Institutes and Organizations across Nations*
Claude Lévi-Strauss's *Structural Anthropology*
Jay Macleod's *Ain't No Makin' It: Aspirations and Attainment in a Low-Income Neighborhood*
Saba Mahmood's *The Politics of Piety: The Islamic Revival and the Feminist Subject*
Marcel Mauss's *The Gift*

BUSINESS

Jean Lave & Etienne Wenger's *Situated Learning*
Theodore Levitt's *Marketing Myopia*
Burton G. Malkiel's *A Random Walk Down Wall Street*
Douglas McGregor's *The Human Side of Enterprise*
Michael Porter's *Competitive Strategy: Creating and Sustaining Superior Performance*
John Kotter's *Leading Change*
C. K. Prahalad & Gary Hamel's *The Core Competence of the Corporation*

CRIMINOLOGY

Michelle Alexander's *The New Jim Crow: Mass Incarceration in the Age of Colorblindness*
Michael R. Gottfredson & Travis Hirschi's *A General Theory of Crime*
Richard Herrnstein & Charles A. Murray's *The Bell Curve: Intelligence and Class Structure in American Life*
Elizabeth Loftus's *Eyewitness Testimony*
Jay Macleod's *Ain't No Makin' It: Aspirations and Attainment in a Low-Income Neighborhood*
Philip Zimbardo's *The Lucifer Effect*

ECONOMICS

Janet Abu-Lughod's *Before European Hegemony*
Ha-Joon Chang's *Kicking Away the Ladder*
David Brion Davis's *The Problem of Slavery in the Age of Revolution*
Milton Friedman's *The Role of Monetary Policy*
Milton Friedman's *Capitalism and Freedom*
David Graeber's *Debt: the First 5000 Years*
Friedrich Hayek's *The Road to Serfdom*
Karen Ho's *Liquidated: An Ethnography of Wall Street*

John Maynard Keynes's *The General Theory of Employment, Interest and Money*
Charles P. Kindleberger's *Manias, Panics and Crashes*
Robert Lucas's *Why Doesn't Capital Flow from Rich to Poor Countries?*
Burton G. Malkiel's *A Random Walk Down Wall Street*
Thomas Robert Malthus's *An Essay on the Principle of Population*
Karl Marx's *Capital*
Thomas Piketty's *Capital in the Twenty-First Century*
Amartya Sen's *Development as Freedom*
Adam Smith's *The Wealth of Nations*
Nassim Nicholas Taleb's *The Black Swan: The Impact of the Highly Improbable*
Amos Tversky's & Daniel Kahneman's *Judgment under Uncertainty: Heuristics and Biases*
Mahbub Ul Haq's *Reflections on Human Development*
Max Weber's *The Protestant Ethic and the Spirit of Capitalism*

FEMINISM AND GENDER STUDIES

Judith Butler's *Gender Trouble*
Simone De Beauvoir's *The Second Sex*
Michel Foucault's *History of Sexuality*
Betty Friedan's *The Feminine Mystique*
Saba Mahmood's *The Politics of Piety: The Islamic Revival and the Feminist Subject*
Joan Wallach Scott's *Gender and the Politics of History*
Mary Wollstonecraft's *A Vindication of the Rights of Women*
Virginia Woolf's *A Room of One's Own*

GEOGRAPHY

The Brundtland Report's *Our Common Future*
Rachel Carson's *Silent Spring*
Charles Darwin's *On the Origin of Species*
James Ferguson's *The Anti-Politics Machine*
Jane Jacobs's *The Death and Life of Great American Cities*
James Lovelock's *Gaia: A New Look at Life on Earth*
Amartya Sen's *Development as Freedom*
Mathis Wackernagel & William Rees's *Our Ecological Footprint*

HISTORY

Janet Abu-Lughod's *Before European Hegemony*
Benedict Anderson's *Imagined Communities*
Bernard Bailyn's *The Ideological Origins of the American Revolution*
Hanna Batatu's *The Old Social Classes And The Revolutionary Movements Of Iraq*
Christopher Browning's *Ordinary Men: Reserve Police Batallion 101 and the Final Solution in Poland*
Edmund Burke's *Reflections on the Revolution in France*
William Cronon's *Nature's Metropolis: Chicago And The Great West*
Alfred W. Crosby's *The Columbian Exchange*
Hamid Dabashi's *Iran: A People Interrupted*
David Brion Davis's *The Problem of Slavery in the Age of Revolution*
Nathalie Zemon Davis's *The Return of Martin Guerre*
Jared Diamond's *Guns, Germs & Steel: the Fate of Human Societies*
Frank Dikotter's *Mao's Great Famine*
John W Dower's *War Without Mercy: Race And Power In The Pacific War*
W. E. B. Du Bois's *The Souls of Black Folk*
Richard J. Evans's *In Defence of History*
Lucien Febvre's *The Problem of Unbelief in the 16th Century*
Sheila Fitzpatrick's *Everyday Stalinism*

Eric Foner's *Reconstruction: America's Unfinished Revolution, 1863-1877*
Michel Foucault's *Discipline and Punish*
Michel Foucault's *History of Sexuality*
Francis Fukuyama's *The End of History and the Last Man*
John Lewis Gaddis's *We Now Know: Rethinking Cold War History*
Ernest Gellner's *Nations and Nationalism*
Eugene Genovese's *Roll, Jordan, Roll: The World the Slaves Made*
Carlo Ginzburg's *The Night Battles*
Daniel Goldhagen's *Hitler's Willing Executioners*
Jack Goldstone's *Revolution and Rebellion in the Early Modern World*
Antonio Gramsci's *The Prison Notebooks*
Alexander Hamilton, John Jay & James Madison's *The Federalist Papers*
Christopher Hill's *The World Turned Upside Down*
Carole Hillenbrand's *The Crusades: Islamic Perspectives*
Thomas Hobbes's *Leviathan*
Eric Hobsbawm's *The Age Of Revolution*
John A. Hobson's *Imperialism: A Study*
Albert Hourani's *History of the Arab Peoples*
Samuel P. Huntington's *The Clash of Civilizations and the Remaking of World Order*
C. L. R. James's *The Black Jacobins*
Tony Judt's *Postwar: A History of Europe Since 1945*
Ernst Kantorowicz's *The King's Two Bodies: A Study in Medieval Political Theology*
Paul Kennedy's *The Rise and Fall of the Great Powers*
Ian Kershaw's *The "Hitler Myth": Image and Reality in the Third Reich*
John Maynard Keynes's *The General Theory of Employment, Interest and Money*
Charles P. Kindleberger's *Manias, Panics and Crashes*
Martin Luther King Jr's *Why We Can't Wait*
Henry Kissinger's *World Order: Reflections on the Character of Nations and the Course of History*
Thomas Kuhn's *The Structure of Scientific Revolutions*
Georges Lefebvre's *The Coming of the French Revolution*
John Locke's *Two Treatises of Government*
Niccolò Machiavelli's *The Prince*
Thomas Robert Malthus's *An Essay on the Principle of Population*
Mahmood Mamdani's *Citizen and Subject: Contemporary Africa And The Legacy Of Late Colonialism*
Karl Marx's *Capital*
Stanley Milgram's *Obedience to Authority*
John Stuart Mill's *On Liberty*
Thomas Paine's *Common Sense*
Thomas Paine's *Rights of Man*
Geoffrey Parker's *Global Crisis: War, Climate Change and Catastrophe in the Seventeenth Century*
Jonathan Riley-Smith's *The First Crusade and the Idea of Crusading*
Jean-Jacques Rousseau's *The Social Contract*
Joan Wallach Scott's *Gender and the Politics of History*
Theda Skocpol's *States and Social Revolutions*
Adam Smith's *The Wealth of Nations*
Timothy Snyder's *Bloodlands: Europe Between Hitler and Stalin*
Sun Tzu's *The Art of War*
Keith Thomas's *Religion and the Decline of Magic*
Thucydides's *The History of the Peloponnesian War*
Frederick Jackson Turner's *The Significance of the Frontier in American History*
Odd Arne Westad's *The Global Cold War: Third World Interventions And The Making Of Our Times*

LITERATURE

Chinua Achebe's *An Image of Africa: Racism in Conrad's Heart of Darkness*
Roland Barthes's *Mythologies*
Homi K. Bhabha's *The Location of Culture*
Judith Butler's *Gender Trouble*
Simone De Beauvoir's *The Second Sex*
Ferdinand De Saussure's *Course in General Linguistics*
T. S. Eliot's *The Sacred Wood: Essays on Poetry and Criticism*
Zora Neale Huston's *Characteristics of Negro Expression*
Toni Morrison's *Playing in the Dark: Whiteness in the American Literary Imagination*
Edward Said's *Orientalism*
Gayatri Chakravorty Spivak's *Can the Subaltern Speak?*
Mary Wollstonecraft's *A Vindication of the Rights of Women*
Virginia Woolf's *A Room of One's Own*

PHILOSOPHY

Elizabeth Anscombe's *Modern Moral Philosophy*
Hannah Arendt's *The Human Condition*
Aristotle's *Metaphysics*
Aristotle's *Nicomachean Ethics*
Edmund Gettier's *Is Justified True Belief Knowledge?*
Georg Wilhelm Friedrich Hegel's *Phenomenology of Spirit*
David Hume's *Dialogues Concerning Natural Religion*
David Hume's *The Enquiry for Human Understanding*
Immanuel Kant's *Religion within the Boundaries of Mere Reason*
Immanuel Kant's *Critique of Pure Reason*
Søren Kierkegaard's *The Sickness Unto Death*
Søren Kierkegaard's *Fear and Trembling*
C. S. Lewis's *The Abolition of Man*
Alasdair MacIntyre's *After Virtue*
Marcus Aurelius's *Meditations*
Friedrich Nietzsche's *On the Genealogy of Morality*
Friedrich Nietzsche's *Beyond Good and Evil*
Plato's *Republic*
Plato's *Symposium*
Jean-Jacques Rousseau's *The Social Contract*
Gilbert Ryle's *The Concept of Mind*
Baruch Spinoza's *Ethics*
Sun Tzu's *The Art of War*
Ludwig Wittgenstein's *Philosophical Investigations*

POLITICS

Benedict Anderson's *Imagined Communities*
Aristotle's *Politics*
Bernard Bailyn's *The Ideological Origins of the American Revolution*
Edmund Burke's *Reflections on the Revolution in France*
John C. Calhoun's *A Disquisition on Government*
Ha-Joon Chang's *Kicking Away the Ladder*
Hamid Dabashi's *Iran: A People Interrupted*
Hamid Dabashi's *Theology of Discontent: The Ideological Foundation of the Islamic Revolution in Iran*
Robert Dahl's *Democracy and its Critics*
Robert Dahl's *Who Governs?*
David Brion Davis's *The Problem of Slavery in the Age of Revolution*

Alexis De Tocqueville's *Democracy in America*
James Ferguson's *The Anti-Politics Machine*
Frank Dikotter's *Mao's Great Famine*
Sheila Fitzpatrick's *Everyday Stalinism*
Eric Foner's *Reconstruction: America's Unfinished Revolution, 1863-1877*
Milton Friedman's *Capitalism and Freedom*
Francis Fukuyama's *The End of History and the Last Man*
John Lewis Gaddis's *We Now Know: Rethinking Cold War History*
Ernest Gellner's *Nations and Nationalism*
David Graeber's *Debt: the First 5000 Years*
Antonio Gramsci's *The Prison Notebooks*
Alexander Hamilton, John Jay & James Madison's *The Federalist Papers*
Friedrich Hayek's *The Road to Serfdom*
Christopher Hill's *The World Turned Upside Down*
Thomas Hobbes's *Leviathan*
John A. Hobson's *Imperialism: A Study*
Samuel P. Huntington's *The Clash of Civilizations and the Remaking of World Order*
Tony Judt's *Postwar: A History of Europe Since 1945*
David C. Kang's *China Rising: Peace, Power and Order in East Asia*
Paul Kennedy's *The Rise and Fall of Great Powers*
Robert Keohane's *After Hegemony*
Martin Luther King Jr.'s *Why We Can't Wait*
Henry Kissinger's *World Order: Reflections on the Character of Nations and the Course of History*
John Locke's *Two Treatises of Government*
Niccolò Machiavelli's *The Prince*
Thomas Robert Malthus's *An Essay on the Principle of Population*
Mahmood Mamdani's *Citizen and Subject: Contemporary Africa And The Legacy Of Late Colonialism*
Karl Marx's *Capital*
John Stuart Mill's *On Liberty*
John Stuart Mill's *Utilitarianism*
Hans Morgenthau's *Politics Among Nations*
Thomas Paine's *Common Sense*
Thomas Paine's *Rights of Man*
Thomas Piketty's *Capital in the Twenty-First Century*
Robert D. Putman's *Bowling Alone*
John Rawls's *Theory of Justice*
Jean-Jacques Rousseau's *The Social Contract*
Theda Skocpol's *States and Social Revolutions*
Adam Smith's *The Wealth of Nations*
Sun Tzu's *The Art of War*
Henry David Thoreau's *Civil Disobedience*
Thucydides's *The History of the Peloponnesian War*
Kenneth Waltz's *Theory of International Politics*
Max Weber's *Politics as a Vocation*
Odd Arne Westad's *The Global Cold War: Third World Interventions And The Making Of Our Times*

POSTCOLONIAL STUDIES

Roland Barthes's *Mythologies*
Frantz Fanon's *Black Skin, White Masks*
Homi K. Bhabha's *The Location of Culture*
Gustavo Gutiérrez's *A Theology of Liberation*
Edward Said's *Orientalism*
Gayatri Chakravorty Spivak's *Can the Subaltern Speak?*

PSYCHOLOGY

Gordon Allport's *The Nature of Prejudice*
Alan Baddeley & Graham Hitch's *Aggression: A Social Learning Analysis*
Albert Bandura's *Aggression: A Social Learning Analysis*
Leon Festinger's *A Theory of Cognitive Dissonance*
Sigmund Freud's *The Interpretation of Dreams*
Betty Friedan's *The Feminine Mystique*
Michael R. Gottfredson & Travis Hirschi's *A General Theory of Crime*
Eric Hoffer's *The True Believer: Thoughts on the Nature of Mass Movements*
William James's *Principles of Psychology*
Elizabeth Loftus's *Eyewitness Testimony*
A. H. Maslow's *A Theory of Human Motivation*
Stanley Milgram's *Obedience to Authority*
Steven Pinker's *The Better Angels of Our Nature*
Oliver Sacks's *The Man Who Mistook His Wife For a Hat*
Richard Thaler & Cass Sunstein's *Nudge: Improving Decisions About Health, Wealth and Happiness*
Amos Tversky's *Judgment under Uncertainty: Heuristics and Biases*
Philip Zimbardo's *The Lucifer Effect*

SCIENCE

Rachel Carson's *Silent Spring*
William Cronon's *Nature's Metropolis: Chicago And The Great West*
Alfred W. Crosby's *The Columbian Exchange*
Charles Darwin's *On the Origin of Species*
Richard Dawkin's *The Selfish Gene*
Thomas Kuhn's *The Structure of Scientific Revolutions*
Geoffrey Parker's *Global Crisis: War, Climate Change and Catastrophe in the Seventeenth Century*
Mathis Wackernagel & William Rees's *Our Ecological Footprint*

SOCIOLOGY

Michelle Alexander's *The New Jim Crow: Mass Incarceration in the Age of Colorblindness*
Gordon Allport's *The Nature of Prejudice*
Albert Bandura's *Aggression: A Social Learning Analysis*
Hanna Batatu's *The Old Social Classes And The Revolutionary Movements Of Iraq*
Ha-Joon Chang's *Kicking Away the Ladder*
W. E. B. Du Bois's *The Souls of Black Folk*
Émile Durkheim's *On Suicide*
Frantz Fanon's *Black Skin, White Masks*
Frantz Fanon's *The Wretched of the Earth*
Eric Foner's *Reconstruction: America's Unfinished Revolution, 1863-1877*
Eugene Genovese's *Roll, Jordan, Roll: The World the Slaves Made*
Jack Goldstone's *Revolution and Rebellion in the Early Modern World*
Antonio Gramsci's *The Prison Notebooks*
Richard Herrnstein & Charles A Murray's *The Bell Curve: Intelligence and Class Structure in American Life*
Eric Hoffer's *The True Believer: Thoughts on the Nature of Mass Movements*
Jane Jacobs's *The Death and Life of Great American Cities*
Robert Lucas's *Why Doesn't Capital Flow from Rich to Poor Countries?*
Jay Macleod's *Ain't No Makin' It: Aspirations and Attainment in a Low Income Neighborhood*
Elaine May's *Homeward Bound: American Families in the Cold War Era*
Douglas McGregor's *The Human Side of Enterprise*
C. Wright Mills's *The Sociological Imagination*

Thomas Piketty's *Capital in the Twenty-First Century*
Robert D. Putman's *Bowling Alone*
David Riesman's *The Lonely Crowd: A Study of the Changing American Character*
Edward Said's *Orientalism*
Joan Wallach Scott's *Gender and the Politics of History*
Theda Skocpol's *States and Social Revolutions*
Max Weber's *The Protestant Ethic and the Spirit of Capitalism*

THEOLOGY

Augustine's *Confessions*
Benedict's *Rule of St Benedict*
Gustavo Gutiérrez's *A Theology of Liberation*
Carole Hillenbrand's *The Crusades: Islamic Perspectives*
David Hume's *Dialogues Concerning Natural Religion*
Immanuel Kant's *Religion within the Boundaries of Mere Reason*
Ernst Kantorowicz's *The King's Two Bodies: A Study in Medieval Political Theology*
Søren Kierkegaard's *The Sickness Unto Death*
C. S. Lewis's *The Abolition of Man*
Saba Mahmood's *The Politics of Piety: The Islamic Revival and the Feminist Subject*
Baruch Spinoza's *Ethics*
Keith Thomas's *Religion and the Decline of Magic*

COMING SOON

Chris Argyris's *The Individual and the Organisation*
Seyla Benhabib's *The Rights of Others*
Walter Benjamin's *The Work Of Art in the Age of Mechanical Reproduction*
John Berger's *Ways of Seeing*
Pierre Bourdieu's *Outline of a Theory of Practice*
Mary Douglas's *Purity and Danger*
Roland Dworkin's *Taking Rights Seriously*
James G. March's *Exploration and Exploitation in Organisational Learning*
Ikujiro Nonaka's *A Dynamic Theory of Organizational Knowledge Creation*
Griselda Pollock's *Vision and Difference*
Amartya Sen's *Inequality Re-Examined*
Susan Sontag's *On Photography*
Yasser Tabbaa's *The Transformation of Islamic Art*
Ludwig von Mises's *Theory of Money and Credit*

The Macat Library By Discipline